WICCA 2 IN 1

FORBIDDEN BLACK MAGIC SPELLS

Create Magic Spells For Love, Lovelessness, Make Money & Protect Yourself From Negative Energies Using Candles & Magic Tools.

Heal Your Chakras Using Witchcraft.

BOOK 1
WICCA
FORBIDDEN BLACK MAGIC SPELLS

Create Love & Lovelessness Spells & Change Your Life With Magic Spells To Earn Money & Protect Yourself From Negative Energies Using Candles & Magic Tools.

Introduction

CHAPTER 1 Spells

CHAPTER 2 Consecrating Your Tools

CHAPTER 3 Magical Money Spells

CHAPTER 4 Herbs to Enchant Candles

CHAPTER 5 Seasonal Spells

CHAPTER 6 Potentiating Spells with Herbs

CHAPTER 7 Healing Spells

CHAPTER 8 How to Make Candles at Home

CHAPTER 9. How can I use crystals to reduce work stress?

CHAPTER 10 Bath Spells

CHAPTER 11.Forbidden black magic spells.

CHAPTER 12 How to cast a Wiccan protection spell.

CHAPTER 13.Summer spells: 6 types of magic that work best in the summer season.

Introduction

When Wicca ceased to be something persecuted in the world, numerous people began to identify with this religious sentiment and because it was the only one up to that minute that had a central female deity as creator. This occurred in the mid-1950s and continued into the 1970s and early 1980s.

Since its beginnings in 1951, Wicca has gained much popularity and has undergone significant changes, being embraced by feminist and environmentalist movements, thus creating the new face to Wicca and worshipping not only a god, but a goddess that relegates God to a secondary position. This makes sense because the spiritual god was worshipped for countless years, while the Goddess was forgotten.

In 1970, the feminist movement accepted Wicca as an "official" religion, discovering in the Goddess a strong figure capable of provoking profound modifications in society's thinking and in its way of seeing the world. This gave rise to many feminist traditions that brought many innovative and quality materials that would change Wicca forever.

Women fighting for the rights of gender equality discovered in this religion a safe haven to feel strong, alive and active. In Wicca they found a religion that could redeem their dignity, both socially and religiously. From the search for a new religion arose, in the United States, a group of thought in which women have not omitted, thanks to the efforts of numerous women committed to feminist causes, Wiccans with a new identity more centered on the figure of the Goddess. From this growing movement emerged diverse customs of this religion, from branches where the God is less notorious and the Goddess works supremacy and prevalence.

Along with the development and scope of Wicca, in the mid '80s, the "rabeira" and some other pagan motions emerged. Druidism, Kemetism, Hellenism, Asatru and countless other neo-pagan movements around the world have just begun to emerge thanks to the efforts of Wiccans seeking to revive a religion centered on the Earth, on the Sacred Feminine, seeking to connect with the banner of the battle for freedom in strongly monotheistic countries, showing that everyone can revere the Divine in their own way, rescuing rituals almost forgotten in time.

Wicca was incorporating Celts, Nordics, Greeks and Sumerians to its structure, these cultures connected with the heirs of the Religion of the Goddess throughout time. Numerous people who had begun to belong to these motions then began to criticize the flexibility of Wicca, claiming that it was not the true heir of the European Religion, that it was not Celtic, that Wicca was an invention of Gardner, etc.

Due to the numerous attacks on Wicca, there was a council with the most distinguished Wiccans of the time to compose the thirteen Principles of Witchcraft published for anyone who wants to read them.

Wicca has been gaining strength and visibility around the world as a major religion in recent years. In the United States and other countries, special forces officers earn chaplaincy, which has been granted mostly and without restriction to Wiccan priests.

Along with this new identity that Wicca was beginning to assume, the importance of the Goddess as the center of praise of this religion was increasingly accentuated. She came to be invoked in the rites as "The Goddess of Ten Thousand Names" -just like Isis, who was all the Goddesses in one-, and the affirmation that all the Goddesses are the same Goddess is accepted among Wiccans and widely used in different segments of paganism.

Wicca then becomes a religion that recognizes the Goddess as the Creator, the main divine being, and although some Wiccans consider themselves polytheists-some consider themselves monotheists, pantheists or henotheists-our religion venerates the one Goddess who manifests herself in various types, names and characteristics.

If in the mid 1950's Wicca was considered more a wonder system than a religion, the current reality is totally different. Many Wiccan groups organized themselves to legitimize it as a true religion, accepting, recognizing and respecting various sectors of society.

The greatest visibility of Wicca is still found in the United States and in Europe, where it is considered a religion of chaplaincy in the army and of marriage relations recognized by the State.

In different nations, Wicca has grown substantially. We see every day an increasing number of literary works that aim to clarify its religious and philosophical elements, and we continually meet people embellishing our sacred symbols, such as the Pentagram or the Triluna, in the subway, the bus, the bank queue or the streets.

Today, many more people practice the Art of Witchcraft alone than in groups called Covens. It went from being a secret religion to a contemporary alternative piety, it strongly fixed the figure of the Mother Goddess and ecologically and socially conscious groups from diverse ethnic backgrounds have integrated much of their culture into Wicca, making it more versatile and therefore eclectic. The saying "All Goddesses are the Goddess" has become a Wiccan axiom because in recent years and so Hindu, Native American, African, Hawaiian, Chinese and numerous other cultures' goddesses were absorbed into Wicca and came to be recognized as different faces of the Goddess.

Most of humanity's current religious beliefs are based on male divine figures and principles, with Gods and Priests instead of Goddesses and Priestesses. For millennia, the value of women has been taken away in many cultures where ladies are controlled and occupy an inferior position to men, either socially or spiritually.

Wicca seeks to reclaim the Sacred Feminine and the role of ladies in religion, priestesses of the Great Mother, and the complementarity and balance between man and woman represented through the Goddess and the God, who complement each other. Wicca gives the Goddess a leading role in both practices, so she is the main divine being worshipped and invoked in our spiritual rites.

CHAPTER 1

Spells

For some spells, you will be asked to chant or declare a mantra or necromancy. These are words from your development or that you have found elsewhere that clearly state the intent of the magic you intend to perform and the result you are requesting. In fact, you do not have to recite something known or known to anyone else in the whole world.

It is believed that there are particular words that you need to state in a specific order a certain variety of times for the magic to work. This is not real and is a misconception about witchcraft. Since the energy already exists in the universe and you simply request its support, you will react and recognize whatever words you always use and when it is clear what it is asking for.

You will also need to use a carrier oil for the oil used in magick, as well as any other type of essential oil. Some oils are too strong to be used directly on the skin, so discovering a carrier oil that works for you will make it safe to use.

Since everyone dislikes different things, some ingredients and herbs cause allergic reactions in certain people. You will need to follow your doctor's advice regarding things you dislike, such as nuts, oils, or ragweed-related herbs.

There are several types of magic that we will use our Herbal Magic four with. Each is identified based on the type of spell it is, some of which are multiple types of spells:

- - Tea.
- - Milk.

- - Food.
- - Baths.
- - Sachet.
- - Oil.
- - Incense.
- - Incense.

Specific spells.

Spell to remove bad energy.

One of the first spells you'll want to do relates to the area you're using. You'll want to learn how to remove the bad energy before you do magic there.

You will use dry juniper to smudge the area by lighting it on fire and asking the positive energy to send the negative energy out of the area. If you are indoors, you will want to leave a door or window open to let the bad energy out.

Increase Good Energy Charm.

Another great Basic Spell to keep in mind is to motivate positive energy in a space where you are going to do an operation.

You will need rosemary, thyme and cinnamon, and for those dried herbs in a cup or bowl, you can use them for incense or put the flame in two. You will light these herbs in the fire and visualize that the smoke emanating from it provides good energy to your space.

Get the person with bad energy out.

Unfortunately, there are times when we will all have to deal with people who are not perfect company. To protect yourself from their negative energy, you can make yourself a protective pouch.

Combine verbena and yarrow petals in a drawstring bag that can fit in your pocket while imagining a force field around the other person that holds all their negativity in itself and a warm white light originating from your center to the area around you. Carry this with you whenever you know you will be around them, or all the time to protect yourself from everyone's negative energy.

Full Moon Bath.

If you plan to do magick with the full moon or in the days leading up to it, it is helpful to take a full moon bath to help you connect with your magick.

In a warm bath integrate half a cup of sea salt, a tablespoon of calendula flowers, a tablespoon of yarrow, a tablespoon of mugwort and five drops of lavender oil. Rest in this bath for at least fifteen minutes to cleanse your energy and prepare for the power of the Full Moon magic.

Amulet or Incense.

Naturally, everyone would like the opportunity to get more money, so use this easy spell to get it.

In an incense burner or Bowl, put a few basil leaves in the center and use a couple of drops of Patchouli oil on them. Light it on fire and chant a mantra asking to get money.

Incense of Enchantment.

If you have work problems, you can use this spell to alleviate them.

You can use incense or sandalwood plants or herbs in a bowl or incense burner or simply use incense sticks or cones. Light it, extinguish it and let the smoke emanate as you shout a mantra over your work scenario. Whether it is finding a new assignment, discovering Harmony in your current assignment or changing an element of your profession, ask for support from the universal energy and you will get it.

Love tea and oil.

If you want to discover love, this tea will help you. However, it also requires making use of the oil on your skin in addition to ingesting the tea.

You should put a single drop of jasmine oil in a carrier oil before using it on your pressure points, such as the wrists behind the ears and on the back of the knees. Drink the tea you've brewed and shout a mantra about accepting love into your life.

Incense or oil for health.

To promote a basic sense of well-being and maintain health, you can use this basic Vitality incense of burning eucalyptus incense or heating eucalyptus oil in a candle warmer.

Lasting love and food charms.

If you currently have a person you like and want your love to last forever, you can take an apple, split it in two, each eat half2, and bury the seeds or core in the grass. This will ensure that your love will continue to grow.

Lost and found bag.

If you have lost or forgotten something, a simple method of casting a spell is to put some almonds in a sachet to find your method.

Night Protection Amulet.

A fantastic method to protect your energy while you sleep is to put some Pine on top of your bed. It can be a branch, a bunch of pine needles or you can even have a pine headboard.

Amulet for protection against hunting.

If you feel that there is any kind of negative energy hanging around your space, you can put lilacs in and around that area to keep them away from you.

Sun Positivity Amulet.

If you're looking for a pick-me-up or a little sunshine on a gloomy day, placing an orange, orange peel or part of an orange tree on your windowsill will harness the Sun's energy and bring it into your home; this will bring healing properties, energy and a sense of happiness.

Incense or parasitic oil.

It can be both real and mental, if there is some kind of bug gnawing at your plants or your energy, any herb from the mint house will fix it. For physical symptoms, you'll want to spray peppermint oil on the ground in the area. For psychological irritations, you'll want to burn peppermint incense.

Break a cursed amulet.

If you have reason to believe you've been put under a curse, you'll want to use hot pepper, even red pepper flakes from the pizza parlor, to protect yourself. Sprinkle the pepper around the base of your bed before you go to sleep, and in the early morning, sweep it up and throw it away. You can do this for as many nights in a row as you deem necessary.

True blessing amulet.

Similarly, to ask for and obtain blessings, you can scatter the flowers of the chamomile plant around the base of your bed before going to sleep. Then, do the same as the previous instruction.

Gut food.

If you have an occasion where you understand you are going to need the nerve to get through it, you can sprinkle some dried thyme on your food and consume it. It can be consumed alone or with other foods.

Incense for relationships and food.

If you are looking for someone to confide in and end up being good and true friends, you can use clove for that. It can be used in food, as is common for glazing a ham, or you can simply burn incense to attract this positive relationship to you.

Communication through the blueprints with tea bag.

Dandelion is particularly useful for this function if you plan to interact with someone or something on a different plane of presence. You can brew a tea with it; they also sell it ready-made. Or you can tuck a couple of dandelions on a lanyard to carry with you.

Enthusiasm and food tea.

If you have a lover you want to infuse with some enthusiasm, you can use ginger for these purposes. You can make a tea with it or use it in food.

Get a sachet for men.

If you are looking to attract a man, you can use lily root to achieve this. It is most successfully used in powder form and usually smells like violets.

Protect other Sashay.

If you want to form a protective barrier for another person, you can use Angelica root in a sachet to give to them to wear. It is more reliable if you also combine it with part of a birch tree, either its bark, its leaf or part of its wood.

Ceremonial charm.

If you want to convey meaning and consecrate whatever tool you are using, spell you are casting, magic you are using or face you are wearing, you can use hyssop herb B to smudge to cleanse, cleanse and uplift.

Cache of protection against nightmares.

Some people are bothered by nightmares, and to protect them from the negative energy of their dreams, you can make them a sachet to place under their pillow at night; in it you can use rosemary, dill and heather to protect them while they are in the plane of unconscious presence.

Sachet to control dreams.

If you have the feeling that someone is trying to interact with you within your dreams, you can increase your ability to experience this by using nutmeg and bay leaves in a sachet that you will place under your pillow at night. This increases your luck and the possibility of having an encounter on this spiritual plane.

Innovative booster sachet.

If you are trying to find a boost in your imagination, you can place sprigs of hawthorn or any part of the hawthorn tree in your work area to offer a boost.

Increase the charm of your business.

If you are a business owner, you can increase the variety of customers you have and the amount of money you make if you place a part of the mint herb over the doorway that the consumer walks through. It is important to note that pennyroyal should not be treated by anyone who may be pregnant.

Wonderful Thought Incense.

If you are working on your spiritual journey and wish to interact through the planes and gain wisdom, you can burn Salvia to clear the space before you begin and help you on your journey to the other side.

Banish the Charm.

If you feel that something negative or an evil energy is connected to you, you can use everyday black pepper and command this curse to be broken. If you were someone who wants to get rid of this energy, just spread the black pepper and circle , while shouting a mantra about attracting the evil out of the person and the area.

Enchantment Diet and Eating Plan.

If you have concerns around what you can and cannot eat and the emotional attachment you have to certain types of foods, you can use fennel to alleviate this. You can use fennel in food, or you can sprinkle it around your kitchen area while chanting the mantra about relieving your food is shoes.

Charm to steal energy and food.

Not only does garlic safeguard against the usually fabulous vampires, but it also helps to secure against people draining your energy and Source of Life. Therefore, garlic can be used to consume in food or bye sprinkle in a circle while shouting a mantra about safeguarding your energy.

Recovery from a broken heart Food.

If you are feeling especially unfortunate and heartbroken, using marjoram in food will help ease the discomfort.

Earth Charm.

If you are about to begin any type of Magickal Ritual or just seem to be out of touch with Mother Earth, you can use enumerated onion powder under your feet if you are standing or under you if you are on the ground. This will help provide a conduit to allow you to become more grounded physically and spiritually before juggling.

Charm in preparation for the celebration.

If you want to prepare your home to more effectively commemorate the upcoming vacation or Festival, you can use a branch or twig from the Rowan tree to safeguard your area. Walk around the space waving the branch and shouting a mantra about safety. When you're done, hang that branch over the door and it will last until the next Festival.

Charm for good memories.

If you are in a relationship and are looking to keep in mind or encourage the positive and good memories you have in it, you can use Periwinkle for this. Taking a Periwinkle flower, you will hold it in your hands and invoke a spell of your development to attract the positive memories you have with another person. When you have completed it, place the flower in a book so that it is pressed and protected.

Remembering those who have passed the incense.

If you are honoring or remembering someone who has passed, a very common way to do this is to light acacia incense. You can use any part of this tree, the leaves or twigs. It is understood that this shrub and tree are associated with both Judaism and Christianity, making it a particularly effective spell.

Communicate with those who have passed the incantation.

Suppose you have a seance or interaction of any kind with people from various realms. In that case, you can use African black wood to increase your avenues of interaction and safeguard yourself when you reach the other realm. By simply holding a twig or a black wood of this type of wood, you will use it as a channel.

Lovely healing spaces after emergencies.

If there was an emergency situation or traumatic event in an area, whether it was a natural disaster or a man-made disaster, you can use the wood of the ailanthus tree to help heal that space. If you build a fire with this wood, you can chant a necromancy to send healing from the world to that environment.

Resurrection Amulet.

This is not advised for any witch who is new to the religion, but it is one of the most well known spells in witchcraft. If one is trying to resurrect someone or something to life, the use of alder wood, specifically in the form of a wand, is the best way to do it. However, because it is really powerful and can also be unpredictable, this is not suggested.

Tea for tension.

If you are looking for a quick fix for excessive tension in your life, you can brew a tea with chamomile, hops and valerian root. This will help create calm in your life. If you want, you can also include a drop of lavender.

Divine tea

Suppose you want to prepare for a particularly strenuous magical spell in which you look to other planes of existence. In that case you can prepare a tea using any type of caffeinated leaf, mugwort, any part of a rose and lemon balm. This will help you provide the energy, concentration and spiritual guidance to cross the planes.

Protective Tea

If you seem to be physically or spiritually secured, you can use any type of tea with caffeine, valerian root, hyssop and comfrey to give you a level of defense.

Earth tea

If you are looking to be more connected to the earth and your life or magick, you can brew this talked about and delicious tea. Using any type of caffeinated tea leaf, hibiscus, hyssop, chamomile, chamomile, hops, rose and linden, you will be using many elements of the environment that will help you become one with it.

To purify the tea

If you find that you need to cleanse yourself before a ritual or if you have something attached to you, you can create a tea to cleanse yourself. Using any type of tea with caffeine, chamomile, valerian root, hyssop and fennel will help you cleanse your spirit.

Clairvoyant Tea

If you are trying to interact across different planes of existence, you can use this tea to do so. Use a mint-based tea, including rosemary, thyme and mugwort. This will aid in your ability to reach other worlds.

Cold and flu relief tea.

To recover from a cold or the flu, you can create a natural tea that does not include caffeine by combining chamomile, ginger, valerian root, dandelion, lemon balm and peppermint. This will revitalize your senses and offer healing and peace.

Fever tea

If you want to relieve fever, you can prepare a natural caffeine-free tea with cinnamon, marjoram, thyme and ginger.

Tea for muscle pain

If you want to relieve muscle discomfort or cramps, you can prepare a caffeine-free infusion with chamomile, valerian root and ginger.

Tea to calm the stomach

If you are looking for a method to soothe an upset stomach, you can create this caffeine-free tea using peppermint leaves, ginger, chamomile and marjoram.

Cough tea

If you're looking to get rid of a cough, you can prepare a tea using peppermint leaves, yarrow and a drop of cinnamon stick.

Natural energizing tea

If you are looking for a natural stimulating tea without caffeine, you can prepare it with orange peels, ginger, cinnamon, lemon balm and coriander.

Tea for a good night's sleep

If your goal is to sleep well and motivate good dreams, you can prepare a tea with mint leaves, hibiscus, chamomile and valerian root.

Tea for food digestion

If you are looking for an easy and effective way to improve your digestion after eating, you can prepare a very basic T using only fennel seeds. It's simple but timeless.

Sensual Tea

If you are looking for a romantic tea to drink with your partner, you can prepare this tea. You will have a very passionate and beautiful caffeine-free tea using mint leaves, rose petals or rosehip oil, orange peel and cinnamon.

Tea of sadness

If you are looking to get rid of sadness, you can prepare this caffeine-free tea that will help you cheer up. Take nettle leaves, St. John's wort, peppermint leaves and cinnamon. This will help your spirit and energy.

Nighttime relaxation tea

If you simply want to have a lovely nighttime routine, you can create this tea to help you in your ritual. Use peppermint leaves, chamomile, lemon verbena, a drop of lavender and a drop of rosehip oil. When brewed, it will remind you of a walk in a cool French garden at sunset.

Tea for sleep disorders

If you have trouble falling asleep, you can prepare this natural infusion without caffeine just for these occasions. Combine peppermint leaves, chamomile and verbena root or leaves to lull you to sleep.

Migraine Tea

If you struggle with migraines, a good natural solution would be to prepare this type of tea on your own. Combine valerian root, linden flowers or linden berries, juniper berries and St. John's wort.

Anxiety Tea

If you struggle with anxiety, a good way to calm your nerves is to brew this type of tea. It combines chamomile, hops, St. John's wort, a drop of jasmine oil and a drop of lavender.

Tea for nausea

If you feel sick or sick to your stomach, you can prepare this tea to calm it down. It uses chamomile, cloves and ginger.

Tea for stomach knots

If you are anxious about something and your stomach is in knots, you can prepare this tea to relax. Use lemon balm, angelica and fennel seeds, plus lemon and lemon balm, if desired.

Bath of happiness

If you feel the need to invite more happiness into your life, you can include these things to your bath: rose petals, jasmine flowers, Epsom salt, lavender flowers, orange peels. If you don't have the actual flowers of any of these things, you can substitute other types of flowers or the oils of those things. Shout a cheerful incantation as you soak in the water.

Bath for sore muscles

If you are overworked or just feel discomfort in your body, you can prepare yourself a healing and magical bath. Include Epsom salt, sage, lavender, eucalyptus and peppermint in the water to soothe your body. You can use the leaves or flowers of any of them in addition to their oils.

Bath to improve circulation

To improve blood circulation in the body, you can take a warm bath and add nettle, calendula flowers and ginger. You can use the root or powder of any of them.

Bath to soothe the skin

If you feel inflamed or irritated skin, you can take a bath to remove this pain. Add to the water any part of alder, dandelion and those indicated.

Love bath

If you want to attract more love and romance into your life, you can take an amazing bath by adding lavender, rosemary, mint and time to your bath.

Renewal Bath

If you want to refresh and restore your energy by worrying about something in particular, you can use this extremely effective bath. Add rose petals, cinnamon and eucalyptus to the water to renew the energy around you.

Career bath

If your goal is to change careers, gain information within a task or find a new task, you can take this bath. Include rosemary leaves and cinnamon while chanting a mantra asking for help with your career.

Green magic bath

If you are looking to increase your connection and build trust with any type of divine being or Mother Earth that commemorates the earth and grounding, you can create this bath on your own. Use lavender, rosemary, peppermint leaves, rose petals, lemon balm, orange peels, lavender oil, patchouli oil and rose oil to develop Bounty around you in the water unofficially.

Milk for insomnia

If you are trying to find a way to prevent insomnia at night, you can develop this Luna magic milk to help you. Using any type of milk you choose, including cinnamon, turmeric, cardamom, ginger, nutmeg and black pepper to prepare your body to sleep early.

Sweet Dreams Milk

If you want to attract sweet and loving dreams for yourself tonight, you can prepare this Milk. Use any kind of milk you like, add lavender petals and vanilla.

Warm Milk

If your goal is simply to get warm and comfortable during the night, you can prepare this infusion. Use any type of milk you choose, add ginger, cinnamon oh, and cardamom.

Milk to sleep in spring

If you want to find a fresh and light way to end the night, you can prepare this milk. Using dried chamomile flowers and vanilla, it's a wonderful way to sleep.

Milk of love

If you want to invest your night in attracting love to you, you can drink this milk of love before going to bed. With hibiscus, vanilla, rose, cinnamon and nutmeg, plus the milk of your choice, it will help you attract love into your life.

Purity oil

If you are looking for an oil for cleansing rituals of a tool, you can make it by including juniper oil, cedarwood oil and lavender.

Consecration oil

If you want to start a ritual with as much magical power as possible, you can use this oil for your tools to modify the space. Add cinnamon, myrrh and incense.

Blessing oil

If you are performing a ritual and requesting a true blessing or if you are simply working a spell on your own, you can use this on any tools, Babs, or areas. It combines patchouli, orange, and sandalwood.

Defense Oil

If you feel negative energy in your space, you can use this around yourself, the space, or another individual. Combine patchouli, mugwort, lavender, birch and hyssop.

Gratitude Oil

If you wish to reveal your gratitude to someone or something on any plane, you can make this oil for that ritual. It combines rose, cinnamon and clover.

Oil To Generate More Income

If you are trying to find a way to attract more funds into your life, you can use this concoction to do so. It combines orange, ginger, sandalwood and patchouli to produce this money or funds attraction.

Breathing Relief Oil

If you are congested or have trouble breathing, you can combine these oils to create a spell. Add peppermint, eucalyptus and benzoin to hot water and breathe in the magical vapor.

Oil of Desire

If you are trying to find a way to initiate lust for itself in another individual, you can use earth for those bells. Combine caraway, vanilla, cinnamon, rose and ginger.

Oil of Enthusiasm

If you want to produce passion in a relationship you already have, you can use this oil in a spell. It combines cardamom, chili, ginseng and jasmine.

Joint oil

If you have joint pain or problems, then this will help you find relief. It combines chamomile, peppermint and comfrey. It can be used topically for a spell.

Relationship Oil

If you are looking to improve your relationship with another person, you can create an earth to help you. Combine coriander, beech, cherry and rosehip oil to use in a spell.

Harmony Oil

If you're looking to communicate across multiple planes, you'll want to make sure everything is in harmony so you don't bring any negative energy with you. You can make an oil that blends cypress, elderberry, eucalyptus, myrrh and frankincense for these routines.

Attraction oil

If you want to attract a partner, you can increase your attractiveness by using this oil in a spell. It combines dragon's blood, lemon verbena and juniper.

Oil of the underworld

If you want to do work with the afterlife and other planes of presence, particularly communication with the dead, you will want to produce an oil to increase your effectiveness and defense. Combine parsley, patchouli, cedarwood and fir oils for these routines and spells.

Open Heart Incense

If you wish to make yourself more open and welcoming to the world of love, you can create this incense to accomplish that. It combines juniper, dragon's blood, dried orange leaves, myrrh, rose petals and sassafras.

House of Pleasure Incense

If you want to produce a safe and happy place in your home and in the homes of others, you can create this incense to achieve it. It combines sage, dried linden leaves, honeysuckle and ivy.

Pure incense for the home

If you want to cleanse a home or an area of any negative energy that you think may have been attracted or attached to it, you can create this incense to accomplish this. It combines myrrh, frankincense, dragon's blood, dill, rose petals and sandalwood.

Rejuvenating incense

If you're looking to fill an area with a sense of renewal and freshness, you can create this incense to set the mood. It combines sandalwood, lemon verbena, verbena, cinnamon and bay leaf.

Incense to eliminate negativity

If you feel that there is a negative energy in a place, you can use this incense to cleanse the space. It combines bay leaves, cloves, marjoram, oregano and Time.

Incense to end attachments

If you want to send away an attachment that is attached to a person or a thing or an area, you can use this incense for those erasing purposes. It combines cinnamon, myrrh, bay leaves and rose petals.

Enduring Love Incense

If you want to have an everlasting love with your partner, you can create this incense to burn at night. It combines vanilla, wintergreen, mint and jasmine.

True Blessing Incense

If you are looking to bless an area for personal factors or before a ritual, you can use this incense for that purpose. Combine lavender, hyssop, basil and the leaves of a flowering plant, such as orange leaves, lemon leaves, apple leaves or cherry leaves.

Incense to remove evil spells

If you believe an evil spell has been placed on someone or something, you can use this incense to reverse the spell. It combines clove, frankincense, skin and holly.

Peace incense

If you want to promote a sense of peace and harmony in a space, you can create this innocence. Combine lavender, lemon, lily root and cardamom.

Spiritual Protection Incense

If you want to find security when interacting on various planes, you can use this incense to do so. It combines myrrh, cinnamon, bay leaf and clove.

Anti-theft incense

If you have recently had something stolen or if you think something has been stolen or if you want to prevent something from being stolen, you can use this incense to cast the spell around it. Combine Ivy, Rosemary, Honeysuckle and Juniper and use them in a spell.

Psychic Protection Incense

If it seems to you that someone is manipulating you mentally or spiritually, you can use this incense for extra protection. It combines elder leaves, bay leaves, valerian, basil, dragon's blood, frankincense, patchouli and sandalwood.

Growing Love Incense

If you have a budding relationship that you want to see strengthened, whether romantic or friendship, you can use this incense to help move your relationship forward. It combines basil, bergamot, rose, lavender and sandalwood.

Attract Men Incense

If you are specifically looking to attract men to you romantically, you can use this incense to encourage those tourist attractions. It combines pine, sandalwood, lily root, myrrh, frankincense, patchouli and jasmine.

Harmony Incense

If you have a relationship that needs help to be harmonious, you can use this in a phrase to remedy your relationship. It combines myrrh, cinnamon, cardamom, ginger and coriander.

Allocation Incense

If there is someone or something you wish would leave you alone and stop paying attention to you, you can use this incense to divert and dissuade. It combines mistletoe, sage, lily root and bay leaves.

Breakup incense

If you want to break up with another person, or if someone has broken up with you and you want to get over the pain, you can use this circumstance to help that evolution. Combine Gilead balsam, patchouli, lemongrass and dogwood.

Fertility Incense

If you are looking for help in the process of conception, you can use this incense to aid in the procedure. It combines mistletoe, St. John's wort, mandrake and cherry.

Forever Friendship Incense

If you want to make sure that you and your good friend maintain a close and healthy relationship for life, you can use this incense to help with a spell. It combines rosemary, elderberry, frankincense, dogwood and yarrow.

End incense

If you want to help something end or come to an end, you can use this incense to help that journey. It combines lemon balm, bay, willow, peppermint, sunflower and pennyroyal.

Virility Incense

If you are a man who intends to become wilder, you can use this incense to increase your stamina. It combines holly, mandrake, dragon's blood, oakmoss and patchouli.

Business incense

If you're looking to revitalize your business on a flourishing journey, use this incense in the workplace. It combines benzoin, basil and cinnamon.

Money Incense

If you want to discover a boost in the circulation of money in your life, you can use this incense. It combines frankincense, nutmeg, cinnamon and lemon balm.

Self-confidence incense

If you are looking for a boost in self-confidence, use this incense to increase it. Combines garlic, chamomile, rosemary, and cedarwood.

Identity Incense

If you are looking for help to persevere and be determined, you can use this incense to empower. It combines chamomile, time, St. John's wort, oak and willow.

Lucky Incense

If you've hit the lottery or just want to discover some good luck in your life, you can use this incense to increase your chances. It combines dragon's blood, linden, mistletoe, rose and clover.

Success Incense

If you have something in your life that you hope will be successful, you can use this incense to motivate. It combines mistletoe, sunflower, onion, sandalwood, cedarwood and myrrh.

Wisdom Incense

If you are seeking another level of wisdom to enter into your spirit, you can use this incense on that journey. It combines angelica, verbena, clove, laurel, benzoin and sage.

Legal Incense

If you have a legal matter or a scenario with the law, you can use this incense to go in your favor. It combines sandalwood, onion, cascara, St. John's wort and oak.

Basic Healing Incense

If you want a healing incense that is easy for anyone to use, this is a great blend. It uses both rosemary and juniper.

Incense for Sickness

If you are already sick and want to help get well, you can use this incense to get over a cold or flu. It uses clove, juniper, eucalyptus, wintergreen and willow.

Incense for congestion

If you have difficulty breathing due to congestion or restricted airways, you can use this incense to help you. It is used with pine, cedar, eucalyptus and peppermint.

Beauty incense

If you want to enhance your beauty in front of others, you can integrate these to develop and motivate your attractiveness. It combines Angelica, cherry, linden, rose and elderberry.

Hope Incense

If you are looking to get out of a depression and find new hope on the planet, you can use this incense to help you. It integrates time, clove, chamomile, patchouli and willow.

CHAPTER 2

Consecrating your tools

Whether you choose to practice magick specifically in the spiritual area or incorporate your practice into daily life, it is often necessary and appropriate to dedicate certain tools solely for ritual use. When this happens, a consecration ritual is required to give your items their proper intention for magical use.

Consecrating your tools and programming them for ritual use will keep their energies clear and focused, which lends much more power to their effectiveness in spellwork and manifestation. In addition, consecrating your tools deepens your spiritual devotion to the craft and shows the constituents and the gods that you are serious about your practice and want to show yourself and them the respect befitting a true practitioner of Wicca.

Choosing Deities for your Ritual.

Selecting divine beings for your consecration routines is not an easy task. Some may choose to invoke the same divine beings to which one is devoted for all consecration routines. Others may select different gods and goddesses for each tool, based on their particular use and intent. Cerridwen might administer a consecration ritual for a cauldron because of her association with cauldrons, while another goddess might be conjured to consecrate the chalice, athame and wand.

It is essential to be careful and considerate when invoking divine beings for any type of ritual. It is usually considered impolite to invoke deities from several pantheons within the same ritual, and it is common sense never to invoke warring deities to consecrate your ritual tools, lest your objects be constantly at war with one another.

If gods from different pantheons are chosen for different objects, it would be best to maintain several consecration routines for each tool to avoid mixing deities. However, suppose all tools are consecrated to the same deities. In that case, only one ritual will be necessary, unless, obviously, your guide leads you to perform several routines at different times, or if you acquire a new item after the others. Use your best judgment when choosing the divine beings you wish to invoke in your consecration routines, and do plenty of research to understand the best energies for each tool and the most appropriate deity pairings in your rituals.

Conjure the elements.

As with any ritual, it is essential to ask that all aspects be present during your consecration ritual. The components will work with and through each tool, regardless of their uses or associations, so it is essential that all of them be present at the consecration ceremony to become familiar with their intended tools.

That said, some tools will fall more completely under the dominance of one element over the others depending on their uses and intentions. For example, athames and swords are primarily associated with the air element, while chalices relate to water, censers to fire and mortar to earth. Choose to consecrate a product through a ritual. The predominant element of the tool should be present to a greater extent within the ritual to help channel and empower its energy into the product itself.

Throwing a circle.

Throwing a circle is the traditional technique for establishing spiritual space in the Wiccan tradition. Casting a circle forms the backbone of every Wiccan ritual, producing connection and consistency throughout each spell and ritual in one's magical practice.

Before casting a circle, a person needs to ground and concentrate on sharpening concentration and focusing on one's own energy. Before working with other energies, one must initially discover how to manage one's own energy, keeping it calm and grounded at all times during a ritual.

A good grounding and focusing meditation is as follows:

Sitting or standing, breathe deeply to relax the body and clear the mind, concentrating on one's breath. After a couple of minutes of silent breathing, bring your attention to the heart center, pressing your palms against your chest with your elbows extended.

Feel the strength of your upper body as you gently press your palms together and feel the box formed by your elbows and shoulders.

Next, shift your attention to your hips and legs. Feel the strength of your legs and feet, knowing that they constantly support you completely. Direct your attention to the ground, which will allow you to become aware of the earth beneath you. Feel how the earth always supports you and soak in the strength and stability it brings.

As you access the molten, rocky core of the Earth, gradually begin to draw the energy up through your roots. Visualize the red energy rising from the molten lava of the Earth's depths, through the crystal stores and subway currents, up to your feet, filling your body one centimeter at a time. Breathe deeply as this energy fills you completely, and then gradually return the energy to the earth, breathing slowly as it descends to your feet.

The circle can be done through visualization, cleansing, tools such as wands and athames, drums, crystals, feathers or hands. The athame is the tool most often used to cast the circle because of its ability to symbolically "cut" the energy that separates the mundane world from the spiritual.

Some Wiccans begin drawing their circles in the east, in

connection with the rising sun and spring, while others begin in the north, connected to the top of the compass and the association of north with the earth component, which helps ground the energy of the circle. Select the technique that works best for you, either by consulting your specific custom or experimenting with different approaches.

Next, you will need to draw the energy to you to direct it into the circle's foundry. Once you have cleared your own energy and kept it grounded and centered, raise your arms above your head. If you are using a tool, hold it with your dominant hand, which is related to predicting the energy rather than drawing it.

Draw the universal divine source energy down through the crown of your head and feel it charge into your hands and your tool. As the energy builds up, slowly focus it through the ideas in your fingers or in your tool, gradually releasing it as you walk or turn to develop your clockwise, or deosil, circle instructions.

CHAPTER 3

Magical spells for money
How to attract money and manifest abundance.

Money is not the measuring stick for experiencing things; most people consider money, character or behavior, and freedom to be similar. And it is essential to the awareness of our right to flexibility, which equates to our relationship with money, as this is one of the main issues in the experience of life. Therefore, it is not a novelty or a discovery that we have such a strong feeling for money.

There are many patterns of consideration for earning money, how you feel about the concept and the amount of money you want flowing into your account. If you can put these thoughts into an aligned consciousness, you can use the powers of the world, and the sky is your limit on your monetary success. In any monetary scenario, the most crucial thing is to understand where the battles come from unconditionally. White magic can provide your service a new aspect, which will help you bring in more money and shoot you to greater success.

Money Magic

Proper thinking

The absence of money makes you feel fear and discomfort when you think or discuss about it, however the opposite is the case when you feel joy and wellbeing, and consider the prosperity and comfort you will get from it. The dissimilarity is substantial, the reason being that the latter statement produces money and the former statement drives it away from you.

The way your mind believes about money is very crucial and substantial, and the most amazing thing is your feeling for money. Rather than dissatisfaction or absence, which is hard to satisfy at this time, your focus should essentially be on what you need. Framing your mind in the right direction is paramount to your success.

Many are often associated with the feeling of lack of having the right things in their lives. Simply due to the fact that they cannot think beyond experience. On the contrary, if money is restricted and they understand and mention it without taking the maximum procedure to maintain their stability. Extend yourself and leave your identity so that you can fulfill your desire. Improve daily to satisfy your objectives and succeed. Our way of believing creates our life; the method we think manifests our reality. Change your philosophy and be grateful for anything; then you will attract different well-intentioned experiences of gratitude. Such a transformation is wonderful.

One of the most important things is to find balance.

It requires being completely balanced, don't just rely or depend on your inner harmony; strengthen and explore what you build in your ideas or mind. Stay focused on your state of well-being, on your actions. Your health also matters a lot.

From most people's point of view, this will occur from an environment of absence, which is not the case. In numerous situations, people may deliberately require or demand something because they lack it, and as soon as they possess it, they remain unsatisfied, the internal reason being that something is constantly missing. As a result it ends up being an eternal struggle for them because of the imbalance.

As for the sacred, Tyr means success and victory in hunting in the rune of the Norse god Tiw. The mighty warrior and respectable ally in times of need. Tyr is the first of eight in the runic alphabet according to the standard rules. All the strength, blessings, perseverance and determination of this Deity can help you. Whenever you demand the magical belongings of this rune, they will strengthen your determination along with your imagination, so that your quest for the rise of service or your well-paid work will be rewarded with achievement. The rune also has refuge, indicating that this spell is for the needy and should not be used by the greedy. Thus, real success is still possible. Just put in more effort and devotion, and it will be within reach in no time.

To turn on the charm

Time: To achieve your goals, imagine this spell in the course of a crescent moon. Wednesday is the preeminent day as it marks the time and day of understanding and world Mercury. Another important day is Tuesday, which is named after the god Tiw and is taken as the second best choice.

Application of the spell

1. Produce a circle as indicated

2. Light a candle with the following command words. "Spirit of success assures, examines and sustains me".

3. Hold a piece of flint tightly in the palms of your hands, and imagine yourself delighted and also satisfied on your way to your place of work with a bag full of money.

4. When you are ready, inhale very deeply and then breathe on top of the stone while presuming that the totality of what you have asked for will be communicated to the stone. And say, "With my breath, I command strength".

5. Paint the Tyr on the flat part of the stone; let it spread and dry next to the candle.

6. The next day, put the stone in the pocket of your coat or pants and move about with it at all times.

7. When your request is fulfilled, throw the stone into the nearest natural water source.

What you will need

A yellow candle 6 to 8 inches tall if you wish to cast the spell on Wednesday or a red candle 6 to 8 inches tall if you wish to cast the spell on Tuesday. A lighter or matchbox is very important to light the candle. A small stone with a flat surface; it has to be small and light enough to carry in your pants or jacket pocket.

More on success magic and money magic

In some cases, it may seem that everything happens for some specific reason. Those specific people are predestined to be luckier while others seem to be consistently unlucky. These measures are not a simple coincidence. Intentional or not, the occasions are the result of the exact strategies and collaborations of others. We can help you achieve your dreams and objectives so that you can be among the luckiest by helping you make your dreams and objectives a reality.

- *Voodoo Ritual*
- *The lamp of work*
- *Money magic rituals*
- *Success magic, money magic - white magic.*

What you will need:

- *- A coconut*
- *- A candlestick*
- *- Heart meat (you can get it at your supermarket).*
- *- Red wine.*
- *- Oil.*
- *- Bones.*

Get two small pieces of wood or coconut and tie them together as a holder for the candlestick.

It is very important, that you develop this lamp for easy

access later or a link. Cut the coconut in half first, then bring three stones, put them under the coconut to serve as a support preventing it from tipping over. To maintain safety, it is suggested that you place the coconut in the center of a cooking tray, alternatively you can use another tray or pan that has high sides so that the oil does not escape. Never remove the pulp from the coconut, as it prevents the oil from seeping out. If the pulp is removed, the coconut will undoubtedly drip boiling oil, which can be dangerous.

Next, take the bone and press it into the heart meat, as if inserting a single finger into the clay.

Place the heart meat, along with the bone, inside the coconut and then put seven drops of red wine on top. As the red wine drips, express your wishes and call Legba.

Next, pour hot oil over the bone with the heart meat; be careful not to fill the coconut more than halfway. While pouring this oil, concentrate on the lamp and Legba.

Now bring two sticks, coconut or bamboo, and place them on top of each other in an "X" shape. You can join them together with a rope or a candlestick.

Next, place the candlestick in the middle of the two bamboo pieces. Hold the front edge of the candlestick tightly and place it in the oil. Note that the bamboo should be above the oil and leave the peak of the oil wick. Then dip the bottom of the wick.

Make sure that the light is kept on until you get the desired result.

Considering that Legba is one of the strongest Loa, you should not resort to it unnecessarily as it could cause really serious effects.

Steps to follow towards success and money.

Verifiable statistics inform us that lack of money and financial problems are major reasons for divorce and often end many relationships. Experience also brings much to the table and informs us that many with a good life requirement are in a position to find a partner much more easily than those suffering from financial problems.

Here are a few tips that can help you repair your money worries:

1. Develop a positive attitude towards money. Many people are daring and try to be the best they can be, but unconsciously think of money as impure. They also have the distorted concept that when someone is abundant, the individual must be vicious. If these concepts also exist in their mind or thinking, they are unlikely to prosper. Money is typically energy. Money is not negative or positive like people's activities. You have to change your thinking towards money if you want to earn more money (you can try using tools like meditation or hypnosis). You can say and experience within yourself: "I am attracting abundance of money. This energy of abundance is good and I like to attract good things".

2. Establish a method of success on knowledge. Nowadays it is no longer news that it is hardly possible to earn a lot of money doing basic jobs and manual activities. Anything that can be automated will be automated, and automatons and robots perform many tasks. Soon simple jobs like booking clerk or cab driver will disappear. The way to make more money is to be different or special by knowing things that others don't understand, like an expert in a specific field. Invest money in your personal training.

It is important to invest your time in learning some foreign languages; learn about what you are attracted to; you can learn psychology, design or mechanical engineering. By learning, you expose yourself to different people and to new and inspiring ideas that are likely to broaden your perspective. Your drive to earn money will be easier if you do what you love and enjoy.

Many people don't know what they want simply because they don't have a clear and defined goal. Supposing you have thousands of dollars in your account, what is the first thing you would do? The thought of many individuals would be, "If I had that kind of money, I would take some time to explore various countries" or "I would have a big surprise celebration."

Another scenario is to imagine that you have passed away. What tradition would you like to offer to the world? What message would be worth remembering from the life you have lived? The most important thing is to start somewhere despite lack of money or time.

Get to know your target group, learn about their problems and ask about their needs so that you can meet them exactly. Invest in marketing so that people get to know you; build your platform where your potential customers can access the answers to their questions and needs. Don't regret investing money and time in doing things professionally.

CHAPTER 4

Herbs to enchant candles

At the time when man came into the world, the plant kingdom was well established and flourishing. Therefore, it is very likely that herbs can be said to be among the oldest tools of magic still in existence today. Shamans, healers and medicine men have long used herbs to restore physical and spiritual health to their patients. In ancient times, the healing ritual was often accompanied by a prayer or incantation to ask the gods for quick results. This usage was maintained when the world was illuminated by the Sun, Moon and candlelight.

It is reasonable to assert that herbal candle magic has existed since the beginning of time.

Plants draw their power from the elements as they grow, and the components are responsible for producing and sustaining plant life. The tiny seed grows in the soil of the earth. Water nourishes the seed and fuels its growth. The fire from the sun helps the seed to grow and convert its CO_2 into useful oxygen for the air. And the spirit of the air transports the new seedlings to begin their development and continue the cycle. Plants and herbs bring natural energy from deep space, so they are the best candle companion when you are performing your candle magic.

The best method to add their energy to your candle magic is to grow your herbs whenever possible. Start with just a couple of herbs that you can currently understand and go from there. Herbs are not difficult to grow from seeds or cuttings and can easily be grown indoors in pots and outdoors in a garden plot. And growing your herbs will allow you to charge them with your energy from seeds or cuttings. If you don't have green space, don't stress; it's okay to purchase your herbs from someone who knows how to grow them effectively.

You can rub the candle with the herb or let the herb charge by candlelight. You can make a sachet with an herb or herb blend and use it to scent your altar while you work your spell. By using the herbs, you will harness the energy and power of these herbs and use them to boost and magnify the power behind your spells.

If the use of these herbs makes you unpleasant or scary, then don't cast that spell, or you can substitute the toxic herb with a similar one. There are constantly other herbs that can be used for your candle spells.

Here are some typical intentions for which you might be casting a spell and the herbs that will work well with that intention.

Intention and its corresponding herb

Abundance: walnut, blackberry, verbena, chestnut, rice, corn, poppy.

Accidents: Wormwood, feverfew, aloe.

Dependency: Plantago, almond.

Cultivar: Poppy.

Wrath: Alyssum.

Animals: Valerian, nicotiana, delphinium, delphinium, larkspur.

Aphrodisiac: Water lily, agapanthus, saffron, blackberry, garlic, clove, damiana.

Celestial projection: Mugwort, magic mushroom, motherwort.

Aura: Yarrow, pennyroyal.

Infants: Yarrow, angelica, fir.

Balance: Sunflower, alyssum, okra, belladonna.

Battle herb: of the masters

Beauty: Holly, aloe, heather, apple, evening primrose.

Beginnings: Blackberry, saffron, birch, birch, birch, daffodil, saffron, heather.

Binding: Unicorn plant, bindweed, bindweed, indigo, marsh grass.

Blessing: rosemary, angelica, rice, anise, juniper, cinnamon, hyssop, hawthorn.

Blood herb: bloodroot, bloodroot.

Calm: Alyssum.

Modification: Solomon's Seal, Maple.

Giving birth: Geranium, spruce.

Cimicifuga: birch.

Clarity: Angelica.

Clarity: Fir, eyebright, cardamom.

Cleansing: Yarrow, bloodroot, sage, clove, rue, comfrey, rosemary, lemon, pennyroyal, mallow.

Communication: yew, mint, yarrow, parsley.

Conception: mistletoe, bistor, geranium, chestnut.

Self-confidence: sunflower, fennel, motherwort.

Guts: Yarrow, black cohosh, thyme, fennel, phlox, samphire, marsh samphire.

Creativity: Walnut, mandrake, tomato.

Dreams: Yarrow, ash, wormwood, laurel, thyme, damiana, poppy, hazelnut, oregano, holly, mugwort, honeysuckle, mint.

Eloquence: Lemon verbena, cardamom, fennel, chestnut.

Work: Evening primrose.

Energy: Lemon, allspice, ginger, ash, astragalus, chestnut.

Friendship: Evening primrose, cloves, saffron.

Loyalty: Rosemary, apple, comfrey, basil, bay leaf.

Fertility: Olive, oak, almond, daffodil, apple, mistletoe, arnica, chamomile, asparagus, mandrake, birch, chestnut.

Gratitude: Bellflower.

Kindness: Honeysuckle.

Happiness: Rose, basil, pelargonium, geranium, oregano, mandrake.

Harmony: Phlox, basil, marjoram, bloodroot.

Healing: Violet, rose, allspice, aloe, pennyroyal, oak, laurel, cinnamon, maple, echinacea, clove, comfrey.

Health: pine, angelica, pelargonium, hawthorn, oregano, oak.

Home: aconite, African violet, thyme, olive, aloe, basil, betony, chrysanthemum, chamomile.

Honesty: bluebell.

Motivation: Hazelnut.

Perspicacity: Walnut.

Instinct: Honeysuckle, chestnut, goldenrod.

Pleasure: Sunflower, eyebright, pine, marjoram, oregano.

Understanding: Hazelnut.

Leadership: Sunflower.

Durability: Chestnut.

Loyalty: Pea.

Love: Geranium, almond, aloe, forget me not, evening primrose, saffron, bluebell, cinnamon.

Luck: Poppy, allspice, almond, oregano, oak, ash, clove, honeysuckle, goldenrod.

Marriage: Rosemary, apple, rose, birch, birch, birch, marjoram, bloodroot, hazelnut, hawthorn.

Meditation: Herb of charms, acacia, damiana, anise, chamomile.

Money: Rice, poppy, alfalfa, allspice, oak, nutmeg, almond, basil, mandrake, goldenrod, chamomile.

New beginnings: Saffron, birch, narcissus, saffron, heather.

Optimism: Water lily, pine.

Passion: Tomato, garlic, parsley, ginger.

Peace: Violet, alyssum, olive, basil, narcissus, chamomile, saffron.

Power: Acacia.

Prosperity: Pelargonium, alfalfa, laurel, bilberry, mandrake, blackberry, hazelnut, goldenrod, clove, echinacea.

Safety: Bloodroot, burdock, acacia, agrimony, basil, birch laurel, amaranth.

Psychic abilities: saffron, acacia, rue, burdock, agrimony, mandrake, laurel, honeysuckle, bistort, garlic, dandelion.

Purification: sage, birch, rosemary, chamomile, okra, devil's claw, lemon, juniper, lavender.

Relaxation: Lavender, damiana.

Release: Comfrey, chamomile.

Renewal: Thyme, birch, narcissus.

Romance: Tomato.

Dream: thyme, agrimony, poppy, anise, eyebright, betony.

Spirituality: African violet.

Stability: Oak.

Strength: thyme, chestnut, saffron, plantain, garlic, marsh grass, pine, mint, parsley, oak.

Stress: marjoram, damiana, lavender.

Travel: yew, basil, pennyroyal, comfrey, nutmeg, feverfew, maple, heather, lungwort.

Data: Bellflower.

<u>Visions: Wormwood, angelica, marigold.</u>

<u>Wealth: Walnut, blackberry, verbena, eggplant, saffron, heliotrope, honeysuckle.</u>

<u>Wisdom: Solomon's seal, apple, sage, hazelnut.</u>

<u>Youth: tansy, anise.</u>

While there are most likely hundreds of different herbs available for use by those who do candle magic, you will most likely be naturally drawn to the same ones over and over again. These are the herbs that have proven to be useful and efficient for working candle magic.

Sage can be used in rituals to invite new owners you wish to cleanse. Sage is used in rituals where good luck or wisdom is sought; also when working defense spells.

Deep pink rosebuds are used for spells of gratitude and thanksgiving. Light pink rosebuds are used in spells of compassion and gratitude. White rosebuds are used for spells of innocence, humility and reverence.

You can use lavender to make a strong tea to drink after the spell. You will use dried crushed lavender when working spells to promote durability, good sleep, purification, clarity of thought, protection and peace. If you wish to enhance your clairvoyance and psychic abilities, then work a spell using lavender and amethyst crystal.

You will use frankincense in any spell you cast for health, success, pleasure, courage, strength, purification and safety. Incense can also be used to cleanse your altar area and to help cleanse your tools and candles before casting the spell. Incense will be used in spells cast to honor the Sun God or any of the Fire deities.

- Bay leaves - Bay leaves are also known as laurel leaves. Crushed bay leaves can be sprinkled over a burning incense or burned in a cauldron on the altar to bring a wonderful fragrance to your work space. You will use bay leaves when casting spells with intentions of success, healing, stress relief or removal of unwanted negative energies. Mix bay leaves with sage to quickly cleanse the area of your spiritual altar. Burn bay leaves while casting candle spells to cleanse your home of the other person's aura after ending any type of relationship. Bay leaves grow well indoors or outdoors.

You will use mint in spells for rest, renewal, healing, passion, success, consecration, good luck, happiness, success and psychic breakthrough. Peppermint is one of the favorite plants for witches to grow at home due to the fact of the many different uses of the peppermint plant.

- DRAGON'S BLOOD - Dragon's blood is a resin collected from the stems and fruits of the Draconis palm plant. Since the fruits are dark red in color, the resin is likewise dark red, hence the name dragon's blood. You will use dragon's blood when casting spells to cleanse your home, remove negative energies from guests or occupants who have left, repel negativity and evil, protect and cleanse your home, and develop a protective barrier around you and your home.

You can also use it in spells to attract money and wealth, increase nerves, attract love, and add it to other herbs to enhance its own natural power. Dragon's blood is equally beneficial for eradication and healing spells.

- PATCHOULI-- Patchouli is probably one of the most misunderstood herbs because of its long association with hippie culture, whose fans used it for its earthy aroma and its indications of nature and earth. Patchouli has been used for centuries as a commercial element and to ward off insects. It combines well with other fragrances such as sandalwood, cedarwood, cinnamon, rose, lavender, clove and myrrh. Use a few drops of patchouli oil in a charcoal burner or light a patchouli incense to provide a wonderful fragrance to your work area. You will use it in purification, protection and banishment spells. It is also advised for candle spells dealing with money, success and love.

SANDALWOOD- Sandalwood has been in use since ancient trading ships sailed from China to all parts of the world. It is one of the earliest wood incenses known to man. If sandalwood is not purchased as an essential oil, then; it is a wood chip and burned with charcoal to release its incredible fragrance. Sandalwood is used for spells seeking spirituality, purification, healing and defense. Sandalwood paired with lavender will call forth good spirits. If you want to have serene dreams, combine sandalwood with jasmine. And sandalwood with frankincense is used to consecrate tools and candles.

Once you have chosen the herbs you want to have in your home, and have begun to develop your collection, you should pay close attention to the storage of those herbs. It is best to store the herbs in a cool, dry place. This will keep them fresh longer, and the sun will wilt the herbs and kill their strength and power. Excessive humidity and heat will cause the herbs to become moldy. You can store the herbs in the plastic bags they come in or transfer them to glass jars.

Whichever method you choose, make sure it works for you and that the herbs are readily available when you need them.

CHAPTER 5

Seasonal Spells

There is always a time for the winter season and fall. Life and time are continually moving forward and regardless of what you think of them, they will continue to happen anyway.

Carefully mastering the seasons and following what we have learned from them increases the quality of our lives and equally helps us to keep pace with the constant demands of life.

The magic of time

It is no news that the rise of modernism has taken its toll on our way of doing things. If we take a look at different types of calendars, we see lunar cycles or the exact time and, likewise, information about when another season begins. This is good. But this information alone does not have the power to eliminate the value of the study of modern magic and perception. We can look to what our ancestors taught us before their passage to the land beyond; and to the various methods we can use to ascertain the timing of certain functions, such as spells.

The magic of the moon

The night sky is the only reputable source of light and guides and seers always look to the moon for some kind of symbol upon which they developed their daily rituals and life. Each form the moon takes has its own meaning, from the quarters it forms to its fullness.

Monthly. Full Moon Names

January: chaste moon, wolf moon, quiet moon, snow moon, manitou moon, frost moon.

Application: January Full Moon may be the right time to think about the power of silence. This is for your psychological health and not just for meditation. We can hear the divine voice and the voice of our Higher Self much better when we are silent.

February: Soft Earth Moon, Trap Moon, Cleansing Moon, Hunger Moon and Return of Light Moon.

Application: February's Cleansing Moon offers you the opportunity to purify your magical tools ritually (you may also get to cleanse your own aura). It is interesting to note that the Romans dedicated the entire month of February to this type of cleansing.

March: Flower Time Moon, Fish Moon, Worm Moon, Storm Moon, Plough Moon, Seed Moon and Sap Moon.

Application: Those living in the northern hemisphere can use the energy of the Plow and Seed Moon to make their own wonderful concoction. Try to find modest indoor containers for your chosen plants. Bury those seeds in the ground on any sunny day.

April: Leaf Propagation Moon, Egg Moon, Seeding Moon, Rose Moon, Budding Tree Moon, Water Moon.

Application: Take your seeds from the Plow and Seed Moon and put them outdoors when the weather is warm. Or you can also host a party for the Egg Moon where the eggs are used outdoors (bringing in the warm solar energy).

May: Hare Moon, Milk Moon, Corn Planting Moon, Thaw Moon, Joy Moon, Dryad Moon.

Application: You should think about using some dairy products in an edible spell or potion in May during the Milk Moon. Milk has the potential to nourish energy.

June: Honey Moon, Strawberry Moon, Rose Moon, Corn Moon, Fat Moon, Lover's Moon.

Application: During the June full moon, it is always specific that the atmosphere be filled with love. You should get to work on your spells and rituals that support your relationships.

July: Blessing Moon, Raspberry Bualo Moon, Nurturing Moon, Homecoming Kachina Thunder Moon.

Application: During July, the Raspberry Bualo Moon signifies kindness. What signs of kindness do you plan to show your co-workers, friends or next door neighbors?

August: Lumberjack Moon, Grain Moon, Mating Moon, Gathering Moon, Harvest Moon, Dispute Moon.

Applications: August begins with the harvest. This is when you will have to enjoy the true blessings of your efforts if you have been working on an individual or spiritual goal.

September: Barley Moon, Hunter's Moon, Small Wind Moon, Spiderweb Moon, Wood Moon, Wine Moon.

Application: Consider the Spiderweb Moon to support our communication and networking efforts. September is likewise the right month to ask, "What am I connected to and is it healthy for me?".

October: Shifting Moon, Falling Leaves Moon, Blood Moon, Sandstorm Moon, Basket Moon.

Application: This Full Moon has the power to bring about improvements. What are the parts of your life that you would prefer to have changed?

Formulate spells for the changes you prefer.

November: New Snow Moon, Frost Moon, Dead Deer Moon Shedding Antlers, Ancestor Moon.

Application: Has it ever crossed your mind to build a family altar for your ancestors in your home? If this is precisely your thought, install the altar on the November Full Moon.

December: Oak Moon, Baby Bear Moon, Cold Moth Moon, Winter House Moon, Long Moon, Wolf Night Moon.

In urban settings, the modern designations of moons, their meaning and their names might also change all the time. Do you plan to invest up to a year in studying full moon events each month? Find a short expression that describes the activities and energies you seem to most desire and apply the concept to the things of your consideration.

To put this in perspective, let's say your year begins in January with the Being in Moon; then the following names follow.

February: represents the Birthday Moon

March: represents the Thaw Moon

April: represents the Mud Moon (or Rain Moon)

May: represents the Bare Feet Moon

June: represents the Lawn Mowing Moon.

July: represents the Barbecue Moon.

August: represents the Garden Harvest Moon.

September: represents the Children's School Moon.

October: represents the Preparing the House for Winter Moon.

November: represents the First Snow Moon.

December: represents the Holiday Moon.

It will no longer be difficult for you when you use the information in annual ritual format.

Stay at home in January and concentrate on rituals looking for integration and also looking within yourself. April, which comes with rain, serves to cleanse the area for your spells, and you need to dance in the rain, so better your ritual.

Get rid of your shoes and be sure to enjoy the solar magic in the month of May. The following month, June, is ideal for you when you want to bond with the earth. Celebrations are best in July. August represents the harvesting of the first fruits. In September, you should perform rituals for the welfare of your children. If you need to perform a ritual for defense, then October is the month you should wait. November is the month in which you should provide yourself a break from the difficulties of daily life and reconnect with nature and the world around you. December, which is the last month, should be the time to reconnect with family members and good friends. In fact, your lunar year will not be the same as any random individual's. Modify the symbolic values of each month and the name of the month as you become familiar with the change in your individual activities and your environment in general. When done in this manner, the lunar calendar will be a direct reflection of who you are at your core, your place in your people and your spiritual self.

It is a recognized fact that almost all esoteric customs have their own seasonal observance. You have no factor not to follow your own custom because it means so much to you. Take a psychological journey and consider the meaning it has for you. Consider carefully what each season means energetically and physically. What follows here is fairly generic, but it is also a great starting point, as it contains some spells and callings that show the energy that remains in a yearly cycle.

Spring themes, spells and charms.

Spring is one of the best times to restore both body, soul and energy. Thoughts of love, fulfilling relationships and lively relationships present this positive energy. This also represents the time of new beginnings, winds and the Air component. Your significant focus should clear out old energies and allow new ones to complete. Cultivate and believe; be real and honest. Use scents, bells and feathers in your spells and rituals to honor the wind.

"Tickle the Heart" Spring Talisman.

Make a heart cutout small enough to wear quickly. Prepare a plume with a mixture of marjoram tea and rose water. Take the heart between your hands (be sure not to ignore the allegory in this action) and make a mental image of it being connected with the white-pink light that seems to bind with delight. Take the feather in its use and dip it all the way into the mixture. Place it in the heart saying:

"Powers of spring, sing, O my soul!

Let it dance with delight; restore romance!

Tickle my heart; play the game!".

Move this token as close as possible to your heart until you feel yourself carried away overflowing with happiness. Try activating it again when you no longer feel the need for this token. Give it as a gift to someone who is depressed.

Spring spell with festive flowers.

Leave your house in the morning; bring freshly picked morning magnums and a handful of lavender flowers. Scatter them all to the wind as you move clockwise. When the sun shines over the horizon, say:

"Happiness outside, hope inside.

I offer this pleasure to the winds.

As these petals are released.

Give me back my joy."

Summer season.

A great number of activities define the summer season. During this time, we tend to go to the gym, take vacations and even visit people we haven't seen in a while. This time helps us develop more loyal relationships and healthy self-esteem. Listen and be present. Use some resources, candles and incense to honor the sun in your ritual.

Summer energy charm.

To start this, you'll need some golden things. Perhaps, a golden yellow AAA battery is a good choice because it represents the "grip" of energy.

"With the chime of 1, this spell has begun.

When chime 2 rings, the magic will happen.

At the ringing of the third chime, power to me.

Come the chime of four, power to buy.

Come the chime of five, magic is alive.

When the sixth chime rings, power - axe."

When the clock chimes six more times, create a mental image of your token being absorbed by the golden rays of the sun in your mind. You should get to recharge your token in sunlight once you have used it six or more times.

Summer season fires rejuvenation spell.

Leave your house on a bright midday day, when the day is still sunny. Create a mental image of the sun in your mind and internalize it so much that you begin to feel like you are going to burst with energy.

"As the carnations and the laurel begin to glow.

So must my magic ignite.

The flames release energy.

So grows the power in me."

Autumn.

The time of harvest has come. Autumn is the season of preparation, freshness and water. You can make use of tears, dew or seashells to honor the Water element.

Autumn Manifestation Fetish.

Think of a particular person or a fascinating work that catches your eye and that you would like to see manifest at some point. What you will need is an agent of the task, a portable container and a percentage of earth that is plentiful. Place a hand on the earth and say:

" Ops, goddess of success and harvest,

Watch over my efforts to ._____ [specify your goal].

Help me to secure what I have diligently cultivated and sown.

Revitalize this fetish with your existence.

May I. (your name)._____ also reap like the earth.

So shall it be."

Autumn Abundance Spell.

You will also need a collection of dried chamomile. Find your way to the midday water source. Sprinkle the chamomile as far as you can into the flowing water as you make this proclamation:

"Abundance flows to me, abundance flows freely to me.

Here and now I claim success and success."

If you like, gather a percentage of the chamomile from the water and let it dry in a portable beauty.

Winter.

This period is also characterized by frugality and alignment with the Earth element. Take advantage of potted plants, soil and seeds to honor the earth.

Health charms for the winter season.

Make this pack of health charms to rid yourself of those aches and pains associated with winter. Start with bandages inside a box. When the three hours are up, focus your attention on staying healthy while holding the box in your hand.

"Not for wealth, not for love.

All I want today is health.

Healthy mind, healthy body.

With these words, I tend to all illnesses.

When these tokens are kept with me.

Bring vigor; eliminate all sickness!"

Keep the bundles in a safe place and put one of the plasters in your wallet. Use the plasters when you feel diminished. This typifies that you have applied the magic.

Spell to keep winter.

This spell blends energy derived from communication with the earth to help increase prudence in the person casting the spell. Start with a piece of wrapping paper that is brown, earth way. Carefully use the paper to cover the coin. This suggests that you have preserved it. Then say:

"One coin conserved, one coin wrapped.

Help me conserve resources.

Place the paper and coin in a hole you have dug near your house so that the energy of saving will preoccupy you. When spring finally comes, dig up the coin and carry it with you as a saving charm.

CHAPTER 6.

Potentiating spells with herbs.

Obviously, herbs have a lot of power on their own. However, there are a few different tools you can add to your spells to increase their power. In this chapter, we're going to take a look at how candles, crystals, stones, gems, and meditation can add a good amount of power to any spell you're trying to cast.

Let's start by looking at the power of candles. Candles are used in virtually every magical ritual and spell you cast. They can be found in all different colors, and each color will provide you with empowered power in a different place. You can see the use of candles in almost every culture and religion you are in these days.

Candles.

When you start looking at the stories of candles on magic, you will find the spiritual. With their fire, they helped to bring out the darkness. Candles are likewise related to the dead. Some spells focus on candle lights that allow you to communicate with those in the afterlife, find treasures and improve your sleep states.

The exact time when candlelights began to be used in magical practices is unknown. Documentation of their uses is found in ancient Egyptian times. In addition, they have been used in almost every culture and religion since the beginning of mankind.

Candle flames were considered mysterious. Individuals discovered that if they looked into the flame and entered a meditative state, they could reach various levels of consciousness. Some were able to contact higher powers and others claimed to be able to check the future.

Magical candle rituals are exceptionally common. They help manifest love spells, prophetic dreams, insight, knowledge, removal of evil spells and many other functions. Candles are an important part of magic.

Pagans have and always will use candles in their rituals. They are often placed on altars or in the rooms of a casting circle. We often see them used at the points of the pentagram.

The color of a candle's light will influence a spell in different ways. Colors have their own vibrations and characteristics that must be taken into account if you plan to stimulate an herbal spell with their impact. Most people bless their candles before casting a spell. Different oils are used for this purpose.

Depending on the type of spell you are going to cast will depend on the type of oil you use. To anoint your candle, just rub the oil on it and concentrate on the intention of your spell.

Let's take a minute and take a look at the different colors of candles that are offered. Also, let's discuss the type of spells that each color will be best suited for. Colored candle lights enhance magical work because of their vibration.

White candle lights are often used when someone is casting a spell for strength; they are also great for spells when one is seeking spiritual truths. Purification or purity spells are also going to be boosted when a white candle is burned. Many people find that they can reach much deeper levels of meditation when they burn white candles during the process. In addition, you can break curses and attract positive forces into your life with candle work using white candles.

Pink candles should be used when you are casting spells that relate to relationships or love. Pink candles are fantastic when it comes to achieving a state of harmony in life; they can also be used to bring peace to your home.

Red candles should be used when trying to improve physical health or strength. Some people also use red candles in protection spells.

Using orange candles can help provide you with nerve. They help when you are casting spells for interaction. When you're looking for a better level of concentration, casting spells with orange candles is advantageous; they're also great when you're trying to fix problems that seemed to have no solutions.

Orange candle lights can also be helpful when you are casting spells to support yourself or others.

Yellow candles can help when casting spells of persuasion. They help supply the spell caster with increased levels of beauty and confidence. If you need to increase your memory or improve your study skills, using an orange candle can be of great help.

Using green candles during spells for one of these two things will be extremely helpful. Green candles are also good when providing someone with a healing ritual.

Blue candles are quite flexible. They are great to use in spells for spiritual or psychic awareness. People also use them when casting spells for safety while sleeping and peace in their daily lives. Prophetic dreams can also belong to the symptom when casting spells using blue candles.

If you do not have aspirations, using a purple candle in your spells can help you discover it. It can also be used to help maintain authority among a group of peers. If you are looking for additional power to enhance any type of spell, the purple candle is never a bad concept.

While gold candles don't provide as many uses, they are quite effective. These are great when casting security spells. Also for seeking enlightenment and connection to deep space or higher powers. Using a gold candle in your spells or meditation practices will increase the power and ease of achieving your preferred outcome.

Like gold candles, silver candles do not require a great deal of flexible use. They can be used in spells to enhance a person's instinct. They can also help unlock information from your subconscious mind.

Lastly, let's talk about black candles. They can be used in spells to help reduce the impact of the loss of a loved one. They can also be used to remove unhappiness or discord from someone's life. Black handles are excellent when it comes to dealing with negativity or negative energy that is surrounding your life or home.

As you can see, candle lights alone play quite an important role in the art of sorcery. When you add candlelights to your herbal magic routines, the power of these spells will be greatly enhanced. This will ensure that you will be able to manifest whatever results you are looking for.

Using the right color candle and lighting it for the right amount of time is essential. Having spells from the herbal range mixed with candle magic will give great results.

Crystals, stones and gems

Since the time of the ancient Sumerians, crystals, stones and gems have been highly prized. They were found to increase the power of spells. Regardless of whether you were trying to improve your health, game safety, or get rid of crystal demons in your life, stones and gems can help you achieve the desired result. This was true in the past, and remains true today.

Ancient Greek cultures also discovered that they could harness the power of crystals, stones and gems. Many of the words we use to name these objects come from Greek. These are just a few examples of how crystals, stones and gems have played an important role. Basically, all religions and cultures know the power of these three elements.

Their power was thought to be that of superstition. Over time, experiments were done to see if crystals, gems and stones had any effect. This helped revive the use of crystals, stones and gems in magical practices. Old customs were integrated with these new ideas, and the appeal of these items skyrocketed.

Today there are numerous books, short articles and other works that provide teachings on the power of using crystals in everyday life. Crystal treatment and magick can be used to solve a few different problems.

It is important to note that there are some differences between crystals, stones and gems. It is not always simple to figure out what you are looking at, so knowing these differences is important when working on a spell. Gems are made of minerals.

Normal stones will have some power, but they will not look as attractive as gems. Normal stones can be found in nature, and their power can be used immediately.

Crystals are a little different from gems and stones. They always have the shape of a pattern. This is how they occur naturally. They have a geometric shape. The angles of the crystal are in balance. And the order of them is quickly seen in this way. It must be remembered that crystals cannot be gemstones, however gemstones can be crystals.

Of the three categories, gemstones are the most expensive. Crystals fall somewhere in between typical gemstones and gemstones in terms of price. Because of this, many people prefer to deal with crystals, as they fit into their spending plans more easily. You can discover crystals in many decorative pieces like jewelry and vases. When you need an additional boost of energy when casting a spell, crystals are a great option to go for.

There are a plethora of these that are available to you. They can help empower your spells with the extra boost you need to find true manifestation.

You will find that this crystal is extremely spiritual. When your life lacks peace or stability, using the power of amethyst in your spells will help rid you of these burdens. It is also a good crystal to use and strong spells.

Agate is a fairly typical stone. It is fantastic when casting spells of strength. It will help you find the strength of your mind, body and spirit. Many use it when casting spells for guts. It is also useful when trying to gain control of feelings. Exalted emotions can make it difficult to see the reality of a circumstance, so casting an agate spell for a clear mind will allow you to see what is going on and accept those realities.

Purification spells can be augmented by using blue quartz. The type of purification, whether psychological, emotional or physical, does not matter. This crystal is extremely calming and can provide you with the words you need to interact clearly with others.

Clear calcite also has many different magical attributes. Golden calcite can be used for relaxation spells and to help you reach different realms.

Fire agate is a stone that many people use in spells that are for courage. It is also extremely powerful when used in protection spells.

If your life seems to be out of balance, casting spells with Green Jade can be practical. This typical but powerful stone can bring peace to the turbulent nature of life. It can also provide you with clarity of mind, body and soul. It can also be used in spells to attract love into your life. Many find that it also works well when casting spells for courage or to increase wisdom.

A less common but also very powerful stone is labradorite. When seeking a connection to the universe or higher powers through spells, this stone can help.

Moonstone can help provide us with new beginnings. When performing any type of moon magic, the use of moonstone is helpful. If you are seeking higher levels of instinct or are struggling with modifications taking place in life, casting spells that are assisted by the power of the moonstone can help you remedy these concerns.

Many people find that simply having this stone nearby helps to lift their spirits. It also has the power to enhance psychic abilities and help you get in touch with your subtle body. When it comes to astral projection adventures and lucid dreaming the moonstone can also be quite helpful.

Just like what we did with candles, stones can add a great deal of power to your organic rituals and spells. When you integrate crystals, stones or gems into magical functions, you are taking part in their energy enhancement can be quite remarkable. This is particularly true with natural magick due to the reality that all of these elements come from the earth. Their lines of power intermingle.

Being familiar with them and developing a collection will help provide you with the power you require to manifest a variety of different spells. Whether you are working on finding love, peace, success, money, or other desires or wishes, using organic spells combined with crystals, stones and gems will help ensure they come to fruition.

Meditation

We have discussed meditation several times throughout this book. This is due to the truth that it is a crucial aspect of spell casting. Meditation should become one of your daily practices, if it is not already. The power you can develop through meditation is incredible.

When you meditate, your mind relaxes and you can begin to focus on the world around you instead of what is in front of you. When you begin to do this, you will notice that the energies around you can be controlled. You will also gain greater clarity and insight into yourself and those around you when you practice meditation regularly.

Many people find time to meditate throughout the day. It can be done for a variety of different functions. Some people meditate to find calm or peace when their day is not excellent. Others use it to center themselves when they start to feel unbalanced. Certainly, meditation is a big part of magical practices and should be done at almost every stage of spell casting.

Your herbs and herbal spells require meditation time. When your tools for magical rituals and spells have an intention pressed into them, it will make manifestation much easier.

As with all things, if you have trouble with meditation, at first, you will need to be patient and keep practicing. Guided meditation can get your head in the right zone much more easily. Meditation is a practice that has been around basically forever. It is a practice that will continue to exist for generations.

CHAPTER 7

Healing Spells

Comparable to security spells, several spells focus on healing and improving the body. As an effective conduit for sorcery and magic, the value of health in Wicca is often underestimated, so being able to cleanse and recover is essential.

As with many medical issues, witchcraft such as that detailed below is not developed to replace the recommendations of a medical professional, merely to match them. The physician's guidance should always be listened to.

A spell for healing

This is a great spell for those who are trying to foster a healing process in others. As a witch and practitioner of Wicca, you will usually find that many people are interested in the type of spiritual and stimulated healing that this type of witchcraft can offer. Thanks to the power of magic, you can use spells like these to help with the healing procedure.

The first thing you will need to do is encourage your patient to relax. Just as you have entered a meditative state in the previous spells we have covered, you can now show your knowledge by motivating someone to enter a similar mode of relaxation. Slow down your breathing and allow yourself to enter into what is called a "neutral mode," where you are both relaxed.

As you both begin to relax, you should feel positive energies and warmth in the surrounding area. Whether it's relationships, their profession or anything else, motivate them to focus on the best elements of their life, bringing these energies to the forefront.

As you speak out loud, the positive aspects and energies should begin to fill the room with a warmth and strong healing aura. As soon as you are convinced that these spirits are present and that they are positive, you should begin to encourage them to assist in the healing.

Quietly, so that your patient does not hear, begin to list the concerns that are affecting the patient and that you want the spirits to focus on.

Throughout this time, the client should focus on the positive elements of their life and the important things they like to do when they are healthier.

If you have practiced the protection spells in this book, begin to develop the positive shield using an aura of light. However, instead of just protecting yourself, imagine that the light connects from beyond you and spreads over the patient. This healing energy will prevent negative energies from infiltrating your client, but it will also help eliminate negative elements that may hinder the healing procedure.

Continue in this manner. After five minutes, both you and your patient should begin to feel empowered and protected. Thanks to the layer of positivity that has descended upon both of you and the protective guard created, the spirits you have conjured should have the ability to assist you in the healing process.

Once this is complete, begin to motivate both of you to come out of the meditative state. Speak gently and help your patient back into the room now that he or she has been cleansed and protected. If necessary, you can repeat this procedure once a day to attract the best kind of positive energy into your client's life.

During this healing process, the existence of nature in the client's life is highly encouraged. It is not uncommon to find that many people whose healing is slower than they would like have very little interaction with nature.

A cleansing ritual with the power to heal.

Just as a cleansing ritual can be used to ward off adverse spirits, these rituals can also be used to help remove comparable energies from the body and aid in the healing process. When one is stressed by a health problem or is not feeling well, it can often be helpful to make sure to properly cleanse oneself of these types of auras.

- • - Incense to burn (sage, ideally).
- • - A single candle (ideally silver or gray).
- • - A little sea salt.
- • - A chalice or cup filled with water (tap water is fine).

Begin to enter a meditative state and keep in mind that the more relaxed you are, the more efficient the spell will be. For those feeling ill or unwell, this can be a difficult step, however, being able to temporarily overcome a health problem can be rewarding in the long run.

As soon as you feel relaxed enough, you can begin.

As the incense begins to burn and the fragrance fills the room, run your hand through the smoke several times. Let the smoke pass over your skin and watch the aroma fill the space. As you do so, say the following words:

" With the air I cleanse myself."

Next, hold your hand over the lit candle (not close enough to hurt, but close enough to feel the warmth in the palm of your hand) and say:

" With fire I cleanse myself."

As you say the words, begin to feel the negative energies and illness burning and smoldering. Next, take a pinch of sea salt and rub it between your index finger and thumb. Then rub the salt over the palm of each hand and say:

"With the earth I cleanse myself."

Finally, dip your hands in the water and get rid of the salt and the remains of the sage incense. As you cleanse your hands, repeat these words:

" With the water I cleanse myself".

As soon as you have finished, blow out the candles with your fingers still wet and dry your hands. If done correctly, you should begin to feel the sickness and negative spirits leave in the next few days.

A spell for the release of negativity.

If you are still encountering negative and harmful energies in your life, this can have a negative impact on your health. In situations like these, the most reliable option can often be to simply ask the energies to leave.

The power of Wicca is such that it will not only help you recognize these energies, but also empower you to dismiss them from your life properly. If this is the type of situation you find yourself in, then read on to find the best way to deal with these problems.

Turn off all the lights and place the candle in front of you. When it is lit, begin to go into meditation. As you consider the lit candle, focus on the power and strength of the fire as an overall force.

Once you have fixed on the idea of fire, then you will need to say the following words aloud in the space:

"Any energy that no longer serves me,

Please leave now.

Thank you for your existence.

I am now sending you home."

The way you say the words will be important. You will need to fill your voice with conviction, focusing on the power of the fire before you and making this power the tone with which you will expel negativity.

Repeat the words, directing them to the entire room. It may be helpful to visualize the negativity being removed from your body, shedding like a snake shedding its skin. This is the healing process made real, helping you to discover the good energy to recover and expel unwanted energies.

As you continue, you should feel lighter and lighter. Once this feeling begins to come, you can blow out the candle and resume your daily activities as you begin to heal.

A healing spell that uses light.

We have currently discussed how powerful light is as a force and how it can remove negative and harmful energies from your life. As the last step for those seeking a healing option, light may well be the missing active ingredient you require to get the best results.

For those who have carried out the above healing steps, repairing the holes in your aura with light is very essential, so read on to discover how this can be done.

Using the aura creation approach we covered earlier, we will repair the holes and start at the top of your head. Visualize the light resting on the top of your head as a crown, a force screen attached to the top of your head.

As you do this, you will now need to extend the healing light down over your body. As the effective aura spreads over your body, it will begin to fill in any gaps and holes that have arisen that may be causing you problems. Say the following words as you do so:

"I ask that my energy body be filled with pure healing light.

With pure healing light."

Use these words numerous times until you feel confident that the healing procedure has been carried out correctly and that your aura has been repaired. When you have finished, thank the spirits, the goddess and the components, and resume your daily life. If you have been feeling unwell, it may be helpful to duplicate this procedure several times to better repair yourself while you are feeling at your worst.

An incantation for self-healing.

Just as an awareness of the power of Wicca is very important, turning this power on yourself can be a fantastic method to recover from general discomfort and worry about yourself. For this particular incantation, you will be using ancient wisdom to take full advantage of the residential or commercial healing properties inherent in the art of Wicca.

More than others, this powerful spell relies primarily on the skills of the witch. Even if it rules you out much more than a novice, practice and refinement of this spell can be essential if you wish to use Wicca for self-healing. In addition to this, it can be best utilized in mixture with modern medicine, intensifying the effects of medications that your medical professional may supply.

The first thing we will need to discover is this mantra. This collection of words has been given and understood among many Wicca users as one of the best ways to recover a body. Consider these words:

"For Earth and Water,.

Air and Fire,.

May they hear this wish,

Sources of life and light.

Fountains of the day and of the Earth,

I invoke you here.

Heal my mind and body."

Learn them by heart and be sure to use them whenever you are feeling down. The words will help refocus your energies and boost the power of Wicca energies to help restore the witch's body.

Bringing harmony and peace to a polluted space.

While it may seem that the body is most in need of healing when a person is sick, it can also work to heal spaces. Bringing harmony and peace to a space or home can speed up the healing process and ensure that the person has the best possible environment in which to recover.

It can even be used in outdoor spaces, although effectiveness may be limited by both the power of the spell caster and the size of the space available.

To perform this necromancy, you will need potted plants of the following herbs:

- - Rosemary.
- - Thyme.
- - Cinnamon.

If you cannot access these materials, dried herbs and a generic potted plant can be used, although they will not be as potent. The goal is to transfer the power of the spell to the living plants and allow them to grow and thrive in the space that requires healing.

Initially, arrange the potted plants in front of you in a line. If you only have one pot, place it in front of you, making sure the soil is within reach of both hands. Place your palms on each of the pots in turn (or on the dried herbs) and say the following words:

"Balance and harmony,

Tranquility and ease.

By the power of the three.

All turbulence ceases."

Imagine the energies you can produce flowing into the plants as you say the true blessing. The quality of life in the soil is finishing permeating with the healing energy you are supplying, which will nourish the roots of the plants. As soon as the total, you must place the potted plant in the space you wish to heal.

The spell will continue to work as long as the plant remains healthy and alive and as long as there is someone nearby who can enhance the positive energies that exist from time to time.

With these two elements, the plant should continue to provide lasting healing help.

Rank Healing Spell.

Our last healing spell is designed for long-term use. Continue with the spell, and refine your skills.

To complete this spell, you will need:

- - Three large white candles.
- - A photo or image of the person requiring healing (the more recent, the better).
- - A single crystal (ideally quartz).
- - A selection of incense of your choice.

To begin, place the candle lights in a semicircle (crescent) in front of you. The incense should be lit, placed out of sight, and enabled to burn while you perform the rest of the spell.

Sit down. Place both hands on your thighs. Feel your weight shift down through your thighs, legs, and onto the floor. Your weight so that there is a sense of oneness with the ground and the rest of the earth. Feel the healing energies of Wicca pass through you as you breathe in, carried upward as you breathe in and pushed downward as you breathe out. This is the procedure to end up linked to the world and allow your abilities to travel a greater distance.

As soon as you feel the powers flowing through you, it is time to direct your energy. Take your hands off your legs and hold them above the crystal. Keep breathing deeply, moving the energies you have just encountered into the crystal and directing them to the desired client. The crystal is capable of concentrating energy and directing it great distances. Occasionally, you may find that the crystal heats up and increases in temperature level. Do not stress if this is the case. It can often be taken as a good indication, although it is not essential.

As you continue to direct the energy, discover the candlelight as it is exposed before you. Observe the protective ring they can form and concentrate this energy through the crystal. The light produced by these candles is a healing light, which you are diffusing far and wide.

Finally, imagine the client as you wish them to be. Visualize him healthy, enlivened by the power of the Wicca you have sent far away. If you know you are using medicines, visualize that the medicines are so efficient that positive energies are sent to cover them with a warm glow.

With the incense still burning, blow out the candles and remove all objects. The energy you have sent is complete, but allow the positive feelings to mingle with the smell of the incense as it heals the client.

CHAPTER 8

How to make candles at home

The vendor, the village candlestick maker, was a critically important individual to villages and kingdoms throughout medieval times. Since the candle was the only instrument for lighting the house at night, the candlestick that made the candles was kept quite hectic, although some individuals made their candles at home.

Today, candles are more of an ornamental product than a necessity, unless the power goes out and there are no lanterns available. However, in the life of a Wiccan fanatic, the candle remains a necessity. It would be impossible to cast a spell without a candle. If you perform many spells and rituals, the cost of buying candles can be quite excessive. Candles are easy to make at home and, after the initial purchase of the necessary materials, are quite inexpensive. By making the candles at home you save money, you know exactly what is in the candle, and the candle will hold your energy. Making your candles will add a boost of power to every spell you cast.

There are some basics to making candles at home that you will need to know before you start. You can make candles in your kitchen, but you will need something to cover your countertops, such as old newspapers or wax paper.

There are numerous types of candle wax, and you can choose the one that works best for you. You may like one type of wax for one type of candle and another type for another type of candle.

- Kerosene wax - People have been using kerosene wax to make candles for hundreds of years. This product is still the most popular for making candles at home because it is inexpensive and blends well with fragrances and colors. The only real problem with using this wax is that it is a by-product of petroleum, and some people may find that the fragrance of the wax triggers allergic signs.

- Beeswax - This is the ingredient that has been used for the longest time to make candles. This product comes from the wax that bees make to live and produce their honey.

- Soy - Soy wax is made from soybean oil that is mixed with kerosene. It is fast becoming a favorite for candle making. Soy wax blends well with colors and fragrances.

- Gel-- Gel wax is a reasonably new product that is made from mineral oil and resin. It is easy to work with for making vessels and votive candles, however, it must be put in a container and will not work for taper or pillar candles. You can add non-flammable products to the gel, such as glitter or small seashells, but including fragrance oils is not a good idea because they do not mix well with the gel.

You can buy wax supplies in the form of granules or flakes, which will make the wax easier to melt. Buying the wax in blocks is cheaper, however, you will need a sharp knife to cut the wax into small pieces or a grater. Whichever method works best for you is great.

The success of the candle depends largely on the wick inside. If the wick is not right for your candle, it can destroy it. The width of the candle is what will determine the thickness of the wick. A tea light candle will use a small wick, while a large container candle will want a thicker wick.

Of course, you can make unscented candles, but then they will smell like burnt wax. And keep in mind the type of container you want to make container candles in. Any type of container suitable for a hot liquid will work for a container candle, especially old coffee cups or glass canning jars, and they make a good gift.

A taper candle or chime candle is a dipped candle. Here is a recipe for making two taper candles.

Materials needed:

- Candles.
- A wooden spoon for stirring.
- A thermometer.
- Some kind of double boiler (you can buy one that is made specifically for melting wax; you can use a small pot on top of a larger pot, or you can put a coffee can in a large pot).
- One-half pound of plain kerosene wax.
- Color (you can buy liquid, powder, shavings, or pastels at most craft stores, or you can use old crayon pieces).
- Aromatic oil.

Use a medium-low heat to melt the wax, stirring often to help the wax melt faster. When the wax has reached a temperature of one hundred and sixty degrees, it is ready for candle making. Too much scent will cause the candle to burn poorly.

Cut a piece of wick to make two candles. Measure the wick to be the length of the two candles you wish to make, plus five inches. Leave the wick as one long piece. Wrap the center of the wick length around an old wooden spoon or pen. Insert the two pieces of wick into the wax. Dip the wick into the wax just enough to make the candles the length you want. Pull the wicks out of the wax and allow them to run and cool for a minute or two. Dip them back into the wax and let them cool. Continue dipping and cooling until the candles have reached the density you desire. Use a knife to cut the bottom end of the candle so that it is as straight as possible. Hang the candles and let them dry for twenty-four hours. Disassemble the candles and cut the wick to the desired length.

To make a container candle, these are the products needed:.

- Container for the candle.

- - Old pen or pencil to hold the wick.
- - Wick with stabilizer.
- - Double boiler.
- - Color of the candle.
- - Scent of candle if desired.
- - One-half pound of kerosene wax.
- - Bamboo stick or skewer.

Melt the wax using the same method as above. The wick stabilizer is a small round piece of metal that will hold the wick in place at the bottom of the candle. While the wax is slowly melting, glue the wick stabilizer onto the wick.

Place the stabilizer in the center of the bottom of the container and wrap the other end around the old pencil or pen to hold it steady. When the wax has completely melted and reached a temperature of one hundred and sixty degrees, add the color and fragrance.

When the candle has the desired color and fragrance, carefully pour the melted wax into the container, trying to keep the wax stabilizer in the center of the bottom of the candle. Do not fill the container to the top, but leave one centimeter unfilled.

Let the candle sit for a while and then see if it sinks. Sometimes candles sink in the center and form a crater. If this happens, reheat the excess wax and refill the center. Let your candle sit for a minimum of twenty-four hours, then trim the wick and buy the candle or enjoy it.

If you want to make a pillar candle, you will make it the same way you make a container candle, however you will need some type of aluminum or silicone mold to pour the candle into. Warm the mold before putting the hot wax in it, as hot wax poured into a cold mold can develop air bubbles on its surface. When the candle has set for twenty-four hours, you can remove it from the mold and cut the wick.

Candles are essential tools for any witch, but especially for one who likes to do candle magic. And candles are simple to make at home with a couple of the right tools and a little time.

CHAPTER 9.

How can I use crystals to reduce work stress?

By using healing crystals, you can manage daily stress efficiently and improve your physical, emotional and spiritual well-being. Using healing stones to relieve stress in the work environment will ensure optimal productivity. It will also help you prevent your inner stress from affecting your relationship with your co-workers and clients.

Suggested crystals for the workplace.

- Amber.

Amber stones are effective in giving you the courage you need to set the necessary boundaries in relationships. If you are the type of person who is not very good at maintaining boundaries between employer and employee or have problems with your relationships with clients, consider having this gemstone.

- Emerald.

This gemstone represents abundance. Use it to achieve psychological clarity while visualizing wealth and prosperity.

- Amethyst.

When you find it especially difficult to manage a work circumstance or when you want to change undesirable situations in your workplace, amethyst can help you.

- Purple fluorite.

Place a group of these stones next to your computer system to protect yourself from the negative effects of its electromagnetic field.

- Garnet.

If your energy levels at work are a little low, a garnet can help improve that overall energy.

- Blue lace agate.

If you find it difficult to relate to colleagues, clients or people in authority, blue lace agate can help you improve your communication skills. It will give you the courage to speak the truth. Use this stone when it seems to you that your voice is not being heard clearly.

- Bloodstone.

This gemstone is perfect for people looking for more motivation. Have you run out of bright ideas lately? This crystal will help you improve your imagination.

- Smoky Quartz.

The office can be full of emotional vampires, from your toxic colleague to your verbally abusive boss. Use this gemstone to protect yourself from these people who suck your energy. This gemstone will help you become more mentally secure and protect you from self-doubt.

- Citrine.

This stone of success is useful for improving your analytical skills.

- Larimar.

This is the perfect crystal to be used to open avenues of communication in the work environment. Use it when you have trouble listening to and understanding others around you.

- Rainbow Obsidian.

Have you been distracted lately? This gemstone is advisable if you want to improve your memory. It will prevent you from missing important talks and skipping important things on your to-do list.

How can I use these crystals?

You can harness the energy and effects of these crystals to combat stress at work in many ways. As mentioned above, you can carry the stones in your pocket or clip them to your clothing.

Another way is to place the stones on your desk or in a sacred place in your workplace where they are visible to you most of the time. Each time you look at these healing stones, they will serve as a continual reminder to achieve mindfulness in everything you do.

Another technique is to create a healing crystal grid in your workspace or home.

How to make a crystal grid.

Although healing crystals are effective on their own, crystal grids have the ability to integrate all the energies of various healing stones, which produces faster and more reliable results.

The crystals you choose to include in your grid will depend largely on your objective. Crystal grids dedicated to the purpose of health and wellness should primarily make use of blue and purple crystals such as Fluorite and Sodalite. You will notice that the energy of certain crystals communicate more power to you than others.

- To develop your healing crystal grid, you need to select an area in your home or work space.

- Next, write your intention on a piece of paper. The more specific the better.

- Cleanse the energy of the room by burning some sage or placing a bowl of sea salt in the room. This is to make the space right.

- Next, place the piece of paper with your target right in the center of the glass grid cloth.

- Next, take a deep breath and say your goal out loud. In addition, you may choose to visualize your goal in your mind.

- There should be a crystal right in the center of the cloth. To place the crystals around the center crystal, start on the outside and work your way toward the center crystal. With each crystal you place, be sure to keep your target in mind. Remember to place the center crystal on top of the piece of paper.

- Next, activate the crystal grid. This is done using a quartz crystal tip. Starting from the outside, you must draw an invisible line between each of the crystals to link each stone to the one next to it.

- Finally, you can choose to add candles to enhance the result of your crystal grid. Let the grid remain in place for at least forty days.

How to clean the healing crystals.

To ensure the absorption power and energy supply of your healing crystals, it is essential to clean them regularly. In fact, as soon as you buy the crystals, it is necessary that you clean them before using them. This is because these crystals have encountered various types of energies as they have been exposed to numerous environments and have been handled by various people.

- One method to clean your crystals is to simply put them under running water until you have the ability to feel that all the negative energy has been removed.

- Another method is to let the stones soak in salt water for several hours or overnight. Then rinse the crystals in cold running water. Gemstones with water content, metallic material or porous houses such as Opal should not come in contact with salt water. Stones such as Lapis Lazuli and Hematite should not come in contact with salt at all.

- You can also choose to clean your crystals in salt without water. Bury the stones under some sea salt and leave them for a few hours. Don't make the mistake of reusing that salt because you have actually taken all the negative energy out of the stones so you should throw the salt away.

- For crystals that should not be in contact with salt, you can choose to clean them through the non-contact method. This is done by filling a container of crystals halfway with salt. Next, take a glass and dip it into the salt and place your crystals inside the empty glass. You may choose to add just enough water to the glass to submerge the gemstones.

Over time, it would not be uncommon for you to notice that your crystals have cracked. When this happens, utter a prayer of thanksgiving for the crystal.

CHAPTER 10

Bath Spells

Debt Eliminating Bath

This bath eliminates debt, whether you are already in debt and want to reduce it or you are trying to avoid acquiring any debt.

What you need is:

4 ounces of baking soda.

20 drops of bergamot oil

One teaspoon of white sugar

One tall white candle

Warm bath water

Instructions

Introduce the baking soda and bergamot oil into the warm bath water and stir a couple of times with your dominant hand.

Break off the top of the white candle, discarding the broken piece over your right shoulder, and light the rest. Place it anywhere in the bathroom that allows you to shower by candlelight. When a little wax builds up around the flame, sprinkle the sugar around the top of the candle so that it burns out.

Go inside and bathe as you normally would. When finished, discard the top piece of the candle .

This bath can be repeated once per lunar cycle as a defense against debt.

Bath of good service

This bath should be taken if you need help with a specific business. A good time to take it would be before an important meeting.

What you need to make the bath:

3 teaspoons of brown sugar.

20 drops of blue food coloring.

Hot bath water

Instructions

Include the brown sugar and blue food coloring in a warm bath.

Bathe as usual and visualize your conference, or any other activity related to your service or work. Imagine everything happening as you would like it to happen.

This bath can be used as many times as necessary.

Couple's bath

This bath is used to increase the passion between the members of a love relationship.

What you will need in your bath:

A handful of fresh rosemary.

A handful of dried lavender

A handful of dried yarrow

A handful of dried cardamom

Petals of a red rose

Aromatic rose soap (optional).

Hot bath water.

Instructions.

Include the rosemary, lavender, yarrow and cardamom in the hot bath water. Add the rose petals last.

In this bath, in a male-female relationship the person who should get into the bath first is the woman. Spend your time in the bath looking into each other's eyes and making sure that some part of your body is touching at all times. There is no need to talk. This bath works best in silence. The couple should clean each other, using rose-scented soap if you have it. Regular soap is ideal if allergies are a problem for either of you.

When finished, dry off as usual. This bath can be taken by couples at any time.

Third Date Bath.

This bath should be taken before a date if you feel in love and want to go on more dates. Despite the name, the number of dates you've been on is not an issue.

What is needed in the bath:.

5 oranges.

Hot bath water.

Instructions.

Cut 3 of the oranges in half and squeeze them over the bath water with hot water. The other oranges should be placed whole in the bathtub.

When the temperature level allows it, submerge them. Let them soak for at least 20 minutes. Not only will you smell wonderful, but you will feel much better. The skin will absorb the vitamin C, so you'll get a physical boost before your date.

When you finish bathing, rub the oranges all over your body and then get out, letting your body air dry, try not to use a towel.

Bath to look for love.

This bath should be taken when you want to find a new date.

What you need for this bath :

A handful of parsley.

5 cinnamon sticks.

Petals of 3 red roses.

Warm bath water.

Instructions.

Add the parsley, cinnamon sticks and rose petals to the water.

Soak and shower as usual. This bath will make you look, feel and smell more attractive when you go out to meet potential dates.

The parsley, cinnamon sticks and rose petals should be thrown out of your house once the bath water has finished emptying.

Bath to increase passion and love energy with a partner.

Have love relationships with great passion and energy with this bath.

What you will need for this bath:

One ounce of powdered damiana leaf.

Yellow rose petals.

A handful of mint leaves.

One liter of water.

Warm bath water.

Instructions.

Put the damiana leaf, rose petals and mint in a liter of water and bring it to a boil. When it has come to a boil turn off the fire and once it cools down a little, pour this water into the hot water bathtub.

Immerse yourself and relax for a few minutes in the water. Once you have relaxed, you can imagine a fantasy to have sex with your partner.

This bath can be taken as many times as necessary.

Bath to strengthen a romantic relationship.

This bath should be taken to give strength to a relationship that has weak points.

What you need for this bath:

Petals of 5 yellow roses.

5 cinnamon sticks.

5 teaspoons of honey.

5 drops of your perfume.

A yellow candle.

Large bowl of water.

Must be done on a Tuesday night.

Bath water at your preferred temperature.

Instructions.

Put the rose petals, cinnamon sticks, honey and perfume in a bowl of water and place it in a window where it can receive the rays of dawn. If you must place the bowl outside to catch the sun's rays, cover the bowl with gauze.

Any time on Wednesday after sunrise, add the contents of the bowl to your regular bath. Light the yellow candle and shower with only its light.

Immerse yourself and relax. When you are relaxed, think of something in particular that your partner gives you and be grateful for it. It is up to you whether you then give your gratitude to your partner.

When you are finished, air dry and blow out the candle.

This bath should be repeated on consecutive Wednesdays for 5 weeks, using exactly the same candle each week. On the fifth Wednesday, let the candle extinguish itself.

CHAPTER 11.

Forbidden spells of black magic.

If someone walking down the street heard you mention Black Magic, you would realize that the reaction you would get is incredibly negative , but you should know that some people can do Black Magic to create a love or protection spell.

What is Black Magic?

If you have heard the paranoia surrounding the evil eye and jinxes, which is what Black Magic is related to, you would understand why this type of magic is so frowned upon by those who do not have a deep understanding of this type of magic. The evil eye, jinxes and hexes are just a few forms of Black Magic and are absolutely intended to harm other people.

Black Magic, essentially, is a negative force. You are using negative magic... you are repelling pure energy away from you. This is the popular belief about Black Magic.

How does black magic work?

Black Magic towards other people involves forcing your own will upon another person, taking away theirs. When you use Black Magic, you are taking away autonomy, which is something sacred that should never be interfered with.

Black Magic Spells:.

We will now discuss some Black Magic spells, taking a look at how they work, particularly three spells that are meant to be used to influence love. Considering simply how spiritual love is to people, this is totally unproductive. Wanting to do magic on another person choice to have their love is somewhat manipulative and will backfire, you can't force another person to fall in love with you, and if love spells have ever worked for you, it is quite possible that the person you were hoping to influence really doesn't love you and you need to leave them alone.

However, it is still a good concept to understand these processes. If not to use them, you can at the very least protect yourself from the impact of black magic against you by knowing that it should be avoided. By understanding this process, you can protect yourself from black magic.

Separation Spell.

This first spell is designed to separate other people. It can be done when the person you love is in a relationship with another person, whether marriage or otherwise.

For this spell you will need a white and a black candle, sea salt, seven whole nails, or clove oil if you don't have them, a knife, an athame, or a candle carving pin, vinegar, black paper, a picture of the people you are trying to separate, a lemon, a sterile needle, black string, and seven nails.

To cast this spell you must be dressed entirely in white.

This spell will be more potent if you use it on a full moon, however if you can't wait, any night will work.

Instructions

Using your athame or pin, engrave the Algiz rune on the white candle. Now, anoint the white candle with the clove oil, or if you don't have the oil, nail the seven cloves to the candle. Light the candle, casting the intention to keep yourself safe.

Now, anoint the black candle with your vinegar and light it.

With the candles lit, take the photo, and with the knife, athame or anything else, cut the photo, leaving only the faces of the couple and then take the piece of black paper . Then take the lemon and rub it with vinegar before cutting it in half with the athame. Next, sprinkle the fruit with a little salt and then use the vinegar.

Now, take your sterilized needle and prick the fingertip, drawing blood. Place a drop of blood on both sides, then take one of the photos and place it on the peeled lemon fruit. Pierce the photo with a nail and attach it to the lemon. Then repeat this process with the other photo on the other lemon.

With the lemons in front of you, use the black candle and drip the candle wax on each lemon. Keep channeling your energy through the candle until you know you are done. It is time to say the following chant three times:.

"Using the power of my mind,

And without being kind,

I pass this evil wave of energy.

To cause you indefinite pain.

To bring only pain.

Your love will not stay.

With the force of my blood-stained fingertip,

Break this relationship.

With the force of my blood stained fingertip.

Demolish this relationship.

With the force of my bloodstained fingertip,

Break this relationship!".

Next, place the candle and put the lemon halves together using the nails to bind them together before fastening the lemon with string. Wrap the lemon in the paper and place it under your bed. Blow out the black candle first and then the white candle.

The next day, bury the package and candle somewhere out of direct sunlight, perhaps under a thick bush. That night, let the white candle burn until the whole candle is consumed.

A love spell.

Often, people feel cheated, they never seem to have discovered the genuine love, which they wholeheartedly want to have, and will demand their partner to be their great desired love, asserting their own will over the other person. This is dangerous, as the other person deserves to live under their own will, free from the other person's intervention. Now let's see how to use a forced love spell. By doing this, the other person taken to be completely in love with you, completely committed to you.

This spell will need several ingredients.

You will need a red, black and purple candle, clove incense, and oil of calamus, cinnamon and myrrh. Next, add 13 rose petals, either black or a very deep red. Next, you will need several strands of your own hair, and some of your own genital secretions on a cotton ball. Next, collect a photo of yourself, another photo of your future lover, and a sterile needle. You will also need a red string, a cauldron.

This spell will be more powerful if done on a Full Moon.

Take all the ingredients, make a circle, and use clove incense for your own defense.

Anoint the candles with oil using first myrrh oil, then cinnamon oil and finally calamus oil. Place them on the altar and light each one. Now, place the images in front of you and start with the red candle: drop 7 drops of red wax on your image first, and then on the image of your future lover. At this time, think about your loved one and how you would feel if he/she were totally in love with you. Let your thoughts develop energy and infuse it through the candle and into their image. Repeat the same with the black candles and then the purple candles.

Next, place the covered candles facing each other and use the thread to bind them together. You can roll or bend them, as long as the photos are touching and are joined by the twine.

Now, place the photos in the cauldron.

Take the petals and drop calamus oil on each petal. Next, drop each petal into the cauldron while saying.

"Your love is strong, your love is mine forever,

Create a bond, a tie too strong to ever sever."

Now, take your sterilized needle and prick your finger and drop the blood on the cotton ball and place it in the cauldron. Next, put the cotton ball covered with genital fluid into the cauldron as well. Now, you should mix your own hairs into the cauldron.

Put a few more drops of the oils into the cauldron, and then drop some of the wax from the three candles into it. Concentrate completely on the genuine love flowing to you, gifting you. Next, repeat your chant:

" Your love is strong, your love is mine permanently,

It produces a bond, a tie too strong to ever sever".

At this point, light the cauldron. Make sure you are in a place that will not cause problems if it is burning and, ideally, do this outdoors.... By doing this, you will release the energy out into the universe. When the objects have finished burning, let them cool and then bury them, along with the candles, outside next to a tree.

Spell to bring back an old love

This last spell is used to bring back a lover. If you have lost a lover that you frantically want back into your life, this is the spell to use. Remember, this is a black magic spell, and it is dangerous and takes control of your target's free choice.

When you cast this spell, you wish to make sure that the person enjoyed you eventually , you will have the ability to motivate the other person to rekindle old feelings and cause them to miss you. This is so effective that you might discover that the other the other person is looking for you on purpose, instead of you looking for the other person.

This spell will require the following:

An organic chicken wing, a red candle, a sterile needle, some of your blood, thread, wooden matches and a sheet of parchment paper.

To begin, light the candle with a wooden match. Take the chicken wing and use it to trace your former lover's name on the parchment paper. With the red candle, drop 7 drops of wax all over the paper.

Now, take the sterile needle and prick your finger. You will need 3 drops of blood on the paper along with the wax. As you drop the wax and blood onto the parchment, make sure you are focused on your ex-lover. Think about how much you loved your ex and how much you want your ex back by your side. You want to feel that desire building up as energy that you can use to send out into the universe.

Now, build up all that energy in your lungs, imagining your desire filling them, and blow out, blowing out the candle and then say:

" Salima Ratiki Bustako Salima".

Now you will put the chicken wing inside the paper, wrap it and tie it into a small bundle, which you should now bury somewhere outdoors. Take the candle with you and keep it, and at the next Full Moon , light the candle once more and let it burn out.

Should you use Black Magic after all?

Black Magick itself is not inherently evil. It is extremely powerful, which makes its use exceptionally dangerous, but it is not always evil. It can be when used negatively, but that should not be a reason not to use it.

Everything exists in a dynamic between two extremes that represent opposites, which is why we have creation and harm. Without harm, there can be no development and vice versa. Without the old, there can be no young, and vice versa. The idea is that one cannot exist without the other, and that is fine.

Everything must have an opposing force that exists to stabilize all that is outside. This implies that Black Magic is a necessary part of the world in order to have White Magic. Without this Black Magic, you could not potentially practice your own White Magic.

Think of the yin-yang symbol for a moment, you must have black and white to have perfect harmony, it is the same with magic. This suggests that Black Magic is just as legitimate as White Magic, and therefore, there is no fundamental reason to avoid it, as long as you are safe and respectful of other people's free choice, it can definitely be a valid option to use.

How can destructive magic generate love spells?

Now, you may be questioning how inherently negative and devastating magic could produce love spells. If everything exists in dichotomies, where there is damage and production, of course, you can damage love to create love.

Just as there is the natural cycle where there is birth, life and death, you can see a comparable pattern in love. Even if you have destroyed something, that does not mean that you cannot develop from the ashes, which will allow you to form something completely different as a result.

Think of the phoenix: it dies and then is reborn in its ashes, looking nothing like it did before. This is what you are doing you may be damaging love, especially with the breakup spell, but it is also capable of producing a new love, with you. This indicates, then, that Black Magic can create Love spells of its own in its own way.

How Black Magic can be useful

Should he be forced to endure that suffering, that anguish and that unwillingness to move on with his life, all because you are naturally inclined to miss what he loved for so long?

What if that could be accelerated to allow you to move on with what is a truly loving and deserving relationship? Should you continue to wait to not think about your ex-partner, who is hurting you? It would work to end that infatuation once and for all to allow you to heal and move on. By letting that relationship die once and for all, you open yourself up to both positivity and the possibility of a happier, healthier relationship. That relationship, then, would be your best bet for joy, and it would be remiss to tell you to suffer in silence until you naturally outgrow the relationship. No... you have to definitely allow yourself to let go.

Letting go of that procedure would involve Black Magic, wouldn't it?

Maybe you have a mental block that you need to let go of to finally allow yourself to move on to the money and success you know you deserve. Maybe there are petty problems that are destroying a relationship that really shouldn't be, and you decide to use Black Magic to eliminate that problem altogether.

Although Black Magick is inherently destructive, that doesn't make it bad. Fire is inherently destructive, and it is the most commonly used element in this book.

Keep in mind, if you decide to use Black Magick, it can produce fantastic and powerful changes in your life. It is effective and sudden, and when it makes a sudden change, it can trigger some severe unwanted repercussions. The power should absolutely be considered if you feel you are ready to use it. Just as driving a vehicle can be deadly if you make an incorrect relocation does not prevent you from driving to work every day, you should not feel restricted from avoiding Black Magic because of the threat. Just drive responsibly, so to speak, and be prepared. Possibly even take someone with experience to direct you.

CHAPTER 12

How to cast a Wiccan protection spell.

Wiccans are, by nature, fairly peaceful people. When they are attacked by the forces of negativity, they are not afraid as they know how to protect themselves spiritually. And that is when Wiccan spells are cast.

This protective form of magic is all about keeping bad energies away so you can live your life free of worry, anger or unhappiness. And I am happy to show you the details of the spells.

What are Wiccan binding spells?

The spiritual energy of the universe is all around us, hidden from view. It influences the reality of the real world, often in ways we cannot fully understand. These energies although unseen are as real as radio waves, which you can't see but emit an energy.

When negative energy begins to build up around you, it can result in various physical symptoms. Some of them can be:

Negative moods.

Unhappiness.

Relationship problems.

Lack of motivation.

You may not know that an accumulation of negative spiritual energy can sometimes cause these bad moments in life and that's why we turn to Wiccan binding spells.

This type of magic tries to remove that negativity from your life , with the power manifested in the spells you will be able to protect yourself. Think of a binding spell as a kind of magical force field, pushing the bad energy away, keeping it out of your reach.

Binding spells are very effective magic, however, I think it is important to figure out how to properly protect yourself when you are still in the early stages of your spiritual journey.

Why does negativity attack you?

To some extent, negativity is simply a fact of life. Even someone who lives the most sheltered and fortunate of lives learns the meaning of unhappiness eventually.

And this is what makes binding magic so beneficial and essential.

Even when they don't mean to, the people in our lives can often contribute to the negative energy we feel.

You don't need to experience anything particularly distressing either: small annoyances accumulate over time.

Even if you are proactive and improve your life and circumstances, the karmic and spiritual residue from your past can remain. A binding spell can ensure that this energy does you no more harm.

In the rarest of cases, your bad energy may be an intentional spiritual attack by someone who means you harm.

Curses and hexes can affect you, but it is highly unlikely that this is the source of your problems. Most people today are not familiar enough with magic to consider this a common form of revenge.

What Wiccan binding spells are not.

Before choosing which binding spell is the right strategy for you, it is important to consider what binding spells are not. If you are encouraged by the wrong factors, your binding spell will not work at best and at worst, it could actively harm you or others.

Binding spells are not for revenge.

Most people have felt the desire for revenge at one time or another in their lives. When someone hurts us, it is perfectly natural to feel upset and want to right that wrong.

Resorting to magic for revenge is a terrible concept 99.9% of the time.

If you are familiar with the basics of Wicca, you already know why this is.

If you're not so knowledgeable about them, it's still pretty straightforward: it's the Rede Wiccan and the Wiccan Rule of Three, which are creeds that deal with morality and the repercussions of doing magic.

The Rede Wiccan.

Although our religion does not require us to adhere to a formal statement of faith, most practitioners of witchcraft accept these two specific statements as the basis for practicing witchcraft fairly and effectively.

The Wiccan Rede states the following:.

" And if it harms no one, do what you will."

Simply put, many Wiccans think that if your magic harms no one, you are free to do whatever you want.

And when it comes to binding spells for revenge, you can see why this poses a problem - all you want is to harm someone who has actually mistreated you!

The Rule of Three.

When the Wiccan Rule of Three is introduced, the concept of magical revenge seems even less appealing.

Simply put, it is the belief that any magical energy you bring into the world will come back to you 3 times. If you focus on witchcraft that promotes pleasure or prosperity, you should expect those things to manifest in your life.

On the other hand, if you bring up anger and revenge, there is always the danger that those things will come back into your life.

And that's a threat I don't recommend to people.

Handling revenge.

As I've pointed out before, revenge is natural, but that doesn't suggest that it's productive or beneficial. Focusing your magical energies on healing your emotional wounds will be safer and more beneficial to you in the long run.

Releasing anger is a hard process, but it is something I suggest when we cast Wicca spells.

Binding spells are not a substitute for actual protection.

A binding spell is a spiritual option for a spiritual issue. If you or a loved one remain in physical or psychological threat due to problems in your life, I recommend that you take more practical actions to ensure their safety and well-being.

Binding spells are magical, however they are not wonders.

Could you please take all appropriate preventative measures if you suffer from an immediate risk?

Wiccan binding spell preparation and supplies.

The binding spell I am about to show you is strongly affected by candle magic. I believe the candle is a powerful symbol of humanity's ability to master the wild and devastating. Since this ritual is about asserting dominion over the negative powers that affect you, it is an especially appropriate symbol.

The candle you will use in this spell should be black, which is a color often connected with bondage and banishment. Black is a physical representation of this binding power, and nothing can escape it.

This spell also requires the use of silver ribbon. Within Wicca, we typically associate silver with the moon, and the moon, of course, represents the Triple Goddess , our divine mother.

You will be invoking the power of this Goddess to bind the forces of negativity around you.

Conjuring and petitioning the Divine is common in defense spells like this one, and I chose the Triple Goddess particularly because of her motherly associations. There is nothing in the world that is more powerful than the gaze and care of a mother.

Finally, you will need a ceremonial knife for this binding spell. You will use it to carve a sigil into your candle, this produces a third layer of protection between you and the bad energy.

For the uninitiated, a sigil is a symbol used within the practice of Wicca or witchcraft.

Various sigils have various properties depending on their form, and the one I am about to reveal to you is often used for banishing. Think of it as a physical representation of your desire to unleash bad energies from you.

Like all magical tools, your knife will require a blessing before it can be used, it is not the quality of the knife that makes it ceremonial, but rather, it is the act of consecrating it for magical use that gives it this status.

I have included a brief true blessing near the beginning of the spell for those of you who do not yet have a truly blessed knife.

And, of course, always use extreme caution when dealing with something sharp like a knife!

To summarize, you will need the following supplies for this ritual:

1 black candle (preferably a large one).

Matches or a lighter.

Silver ribbon (enough to tie around the candle).

Ceremonial knife.

Instructions for the Wiccan Binding spell.

To begin the spell, clear a place where you can work quietly.

Stand in the center of your space, and, out loud, repeat the following:

"I banish all negativity and bad energy from this sacred place. No spirit of ill will can interrupt my actions."

Now, move to the northernmost area of your location and face north. With your hands raised, say this:

"Protectors of the north, hear my request. Watch while I bind the powers of evil."

Now head to the westernmost point. Repeat the above invocation, substituting "north" for "west". Do the same for south and east to finish this step.

If your knife has not yet been blessed for magical use, now is the time to do so. You may skip this step if it does not apply to you.

Return to the center of the circle. Very carefully, hold the knife horizontally using both palms to support it. Repeat this blessing as you do so:.

"Spirits of consecration, bless this tool to do my will. Cleanse it of any spiritual impurities, that it may be a magical beacon of light and goodness. So be it."

Put the knife back in its place for the time being.

Now you should take your black candle and place it in front of you. Then say the following:

"I am not afraid of the dark. The omnipresent power of black binds that which seeks to harm me. By the light of this flame, I am protected from the corrupting influence of negativity."

Now, very thoroughly, you will carve a sigil on the side of the candle.

To begin, draw as perfect a circle as you can. Draw a straight line from the top to the bottom of the circle. To complete the sigil, draw a straight line from left to left.

Now it is time to light the candle. As soon as it is lit, say the following prayer

Union is my will, the flame is my protector. I do not allow the powers of evil to harm me.

Next, take your silver ribbon and connect it above the sigil, if possible.

If you know how to connect a square knot, use it to have powerful magical properties (specifically for binding). If not, use a lasso or some other easy knot.

Now it is time to invoke the Triple Goddess and her security. To do this, say the following:

"Great Triple Goddess, divine mother of heaven, hear my prayer. The influence of evil is at my door, although I resist it. [Here you should add a brief description of the specific problems you are facing and why you need this binding spell]. Watch over me so that evil does not come upon me any more. I entrust myself to your love and protection."

To conclude the binding spell, stand in the center of your area once again while holding your candle. In a voice of authority, repeat this:.

"I feel the relocation of magic. The bonding is complete. With the help of the Goddess, negative influences and bad energies are banished from my presence."

Blow out the candle to end the ritual.

If possible, the candle should burn for a couple of hours each day after the ritual until it is completely spent.

This will ensure that the binding magic is as effective and long lasting as possible. Once it is spent, it should be disposed of respectfully, preferably by burying it outside.

The candle's power should keep you safe.

Using it for any other purpose will nullify the impact of the ritual.

CHAPTER 13

Summer spells: 6 types of magic that work best in the summer season.

Each season embodies particular spiritual styles and energies that are distinct to that time of year. And summer is no exception to this rule.

Some of the most dominant energies during the summer season consist of:

Enthusiasm

Vitality

Life Enhancement

Strength

Delight

Celebration

Because of these distinct correspondences, some forms of magic will experience a spiritual surge during the summer months. When the goals of your magick align with the energies of the season, you are more likely to experience a quicker and more powerful result from your spell.

. If you haven't tried spells of this type before, summer is the season to try it!

Blessing Magic

As the name implies, true blessing magic involves blessing people or objects by attracting positive and helpful energies. In a way, a blessing is a type of defense; by surrounding the object of your blessing with good energy, negative energy has a harder time gaining a foothold. Regardless of the specific form your true blessings take, they function as a force of goodness on the planet.

Summer is a time of power and abundance, which aligns perfectly with the goals behind true blessing magick. This is the time of year when life is at its peak and the universe has plenty of true blessings to .

Blessing magic is a broad classification that encompasses all types of practices. Some of the most common types are

True blessing rituals
True blessing prayers
Blessing (with consecrated water or oil)
Talismans (physical objects suggested to attract good energy).

Conjuring the God and Goddess.

Using the power of ritual magic, Wiccans can invoke the spirits of the Horned God and the Triple Goddess to share their power or give them gratitude. When performed respectfully and properly, it allows one to tap into the divine forces that stimulate life.

During the summer, the God and Goddess of Wicca are at the height of their powers, making it an especially appropriate time to invoke them. Both share in the life and vitality of the season and want to bestow their true blessings on all who ask.

Invocations usually consist of prayers and rituals to the divine being being being invoked, and usually include some sort of offering , it's something you should constantly remember!

Both the God and the Goddess have summer vacations associated with them, making them ideal dates for an invocation. Traditionally, the Goddess is associated with Beltane, May 1, while the God is related to Litha, which falls on the summer solstice.

Plant magic.

Plant magic is a broad category that encompasses any type of magic that works with the help of plants. It is a type of ancient witchcraft that goes back far beyond the history of Wicca itself , people have been harnessing the magical power of plants in various forms for hundreds of years.

Summer is the perfect time to work with plants because they are a symbol t of the vital power of the season. Just as they are nourished and enhanced by the warm sunshine of the summer season, they can help nourish and empower our own lives with the spiritual power they provide.

There are too many types of plant magick to list them all here, but some types are more typical and popular than others. Some types of plant magick are:

Sachets (small bags of fragrant, dried plants, herbs and flowers).

Tinctures (extracts made by soaking plants in alcohol or other liquids).

Cleansing (burning herbs or other plants with specific spiritual energies).

True plant blessings (to ensure the health of growing plants).

When it comes to plants, it is always beneficial for a witch to grow her own.

Fire magic.

The power of flames is a vital part of many spells and rituals. From removal to actual blessing, fire is a symbol that appears regularly in magic.

Fire is an element of passion and intensity, making it a natural for summer spiritual spells. In fact, fire (particularly bonfires) plays an important role in the event of two of the Wiccan summer vacations, Beltane and Litha.

Fire magic can be used in a variety of ways, from candle spells to bonfires in rituals. And let's not forget the supreme source of fire, the sun. It would consist of rituals that work with or honor the sun as an important aspect of fire magic.

Love magic.

Love is in the air when the summer season arrives, so it's the perfect time for a little love magic. Any spells or rituals having to do with love, relationships or another aspect of love will be more powerful in the summer.

While summer is a great time for love spells in general, some types of spells are best cast at different points in the season.

For example, the time around Beltane (May 1) is a typical time for fertility magic, while the time around Litha (approximately June 22) is a better time for spells having to do with passion and love. Finally, the end of summer is a good time to ask for continued love and success in a lasting relationship.

Prosperity magic.

Prosperity is another magical theme that works well with the summer season. Any type of ritual or spell intended to manifest abundance in your life falls into the category of success magic, whether physical, emotional or spiritual.

Late summer is a particularly good time for success magic, especially around the Lammas vacation (August 1). Traditionally, this was a time when farmers would ask for a good harvest for the fall, however, you can use this period to ask for any kind of success.

The manifestation of prosperity is usually in the form of money spells, but that's not the only thing you can do. Achieving a particular personal goal can be another type of success, so spells involving this are equally a good option at this time. Finally, invocations and prayers to the God and Goddess are common ways Wiccans seek prosperity through magic.

Your magical summer awaits.

Discovering the best time for spells may seem like a hassle, but it is actually one of the most effective tools a witchcraft practitioner has at his or her disposal. When energies and your personal will are aligned to the maximum, you begin to experience the true power of magic.

Magick is not simply a summer affair, it is something you can practice all year long!

Conclusion

Now that we have reached the end of this book, you should know that magic powerful and enticing. With so many different spells to practice and discover, having the ability to discover the true advantages of the magical world is something you should be practicing.

The spiritual world has been found to connect with the world of modern medicine, varying only in its procedures. The magical world is as genuine as the air you breathe. Make no mistake, there are worlds in our world, and they are experienced only through our belief system. This is what determines your degree of success in casting spells.

These spells should be accepted as life because they give you an advantage in our current world.

Looking at the whole universe and its complexity, we will agree that higher powers exist and can be used to our advantage. These spells must be internalized and held as sacred, following all instructions and directions. Some aspects can be invoked to work in our favor.

We are affected consciously or unconsciously by the four elements (Earth, Fire, Air and Water) in nature, which offers a means of interaction with the spiritual source. A positive mind will naturally grow the spirit and body, as compared to a negative and embittered mind, which is constantly in conflict with itself and its environment, and is defined by poor performance. Seek to reside in harmony with yourself first, then you can live in harmony with your environment. Private victories precede public triumphs; therefore, you must improve yourself from within.

Your state of mind will reflect the quality of your spells. Spells help you to be in tune with nature and to awaken inner energies, which integrate with our exterior to provide the desired effect.

Working with spells is based on principles, which are a function of their creation. The utmost caution should be exercised in these exercises and procedures to maintain the results and understanding of the spells.

As a beginner's guide, this book attempts to put the basics of spell casting in your hands. What you learn about one spell will often feed into the others, expanding your knowledge at every opportunity.

With this in mind, it can be helpful to view spells as an ongoing learning process. Difficult to master, there is always another spell to learn and always a better way to perfect your efforts.

Thank you for reading this book, I would appreciate your feedback on what you have read, I appreciate your trust.

BOOK 2

WICCA

FORBIDDEN BLACK MAGIC SPELLS

Create Spells With The Energy
Of The Moon And Fire.

Heal Your Body By Healing Your Chakras
Using Witchcraft Herbs And Magic.

CHAPTER 1: THE ROLE OF FIRE IN WICCA

Fire is one of the four central elements of Wicca, which is used to provide an explanation of natural patterns. There are four primary elements of Wicca that are interconnected. The elements are fire, water, air and earth. Each represents an individual perspective, which is crucial when casting spells and also as a representation of the different seasons of a person's life. Each element has its particular meaning and each participant of Wicca should be able to personalize the feelings associated with each element and understand what they represent and symbolize.

Fire is an incredible element of Wicca because of its ability to affect extremes. First of all, it is clear that without it, it is extremely difficult for humans to live. Today, humans do not eat raw food and must rely on fire for cooking. Although fire is a positive thing, it is also considered destructive and can cause serious damage to the person and surrounding objects. The fire element is the only one that cannot be affected as easily as other elements, such as earth and water. Earth. While the others are not dangerous to work with, fire can make you sick and cause you to suffer greatly. For this reason, fire is believed to be one of the strongest elements and is associated with vital energy.

In Wicca fire is the symbol of the soul, whose source is energy. It can be used as a source of energy to stimulate enthusiasm for the process of creation, as well as obsession with destruction. In general, creative forces transform the form of one substance into another, usually of a positive type. However, care must be taken when dealing with fire, as it is also capable of transforming an element into a negative or regressive form. A good example of a positive transformation is when green raw materials are transformed into food, and a negative transformation is when a house burns to ashes. Similar to our physical environment, fire can be used in the realm of spirituality to draw positive or negative conclusions. Fire forged spells can be used to benefit people or to destroy them. For example, you can employ fire to bring positive energy into your life , or to eliminate anything completely.

Fire is believed to come from the south, although it is possible to invoke it from any direction when casting spells. It is closely associated with the zodiac signs Aries, Leo and Sagittarius, as well as the planets Mars, Pluto and Jupiter. It is believed that those with these zodiac signs invoke fire more quickly. But everyone has a fire within them, and as long as their belief exists, the person will be in a position to invoke it. A very crucial aspect that any Wiccan or future witch should keep in mind is the fact that fire needs to be always nurtured and fed. Just as plants, animals and children are fed to grow and develop, one must always feed the fire of one's soul. It has been said that fire is typically related to action and constant activation. Therefore, you should stop being passive and try to be active, especially when it comes to your passions and creativity.

Once you are aware of the fire in you and the role you can play in making it successful, you will be competent to cast certain spells successfully. The most common use of fire is in spells that are quick to act and powerful, those filled with energy. Casting spells with fire as an element must be done with great caution because the enormous power and energy that the element of fire possesses could have the potential to become and be completely destructive. The use of fire can increase the effectiveness of any spell. This is why any witch or anyone casting a spell employs an element of fire, just as the spells they cast are drawn to other elements. In virtually all spell casting rituals fire is present. This is a testament to the importance that fire can bring to Wiccans, as well as the benefits derived from its use in every spell work.

If we consider the idea and concept behind the use of candles in the Wiccan ceremony, it might be necessary to remember that the more intention and personality put into the candle, the greater the energy and strength. If magic runs through the candles once the intention is set and then ignited by the flame. Candace Looft, practical witch, candle maker and astrologer, states that lighting candles is the simplest and oldest method you can use to tell the universe the things you would like to hear.

Candles are said to be a representation of the four main elements of witchcraft. The wicks and their base are symbols of the Earth that are designed to ensure that the candle holds steady. The wax melts and transforms into liquid and solid. This is why it is believed to be a symbol of water. Fire cannot exist without oxygen. This means that the air element is present and functioning within the candle. The flame, in turn, is the fire, and completes all the elements of Wicca. Certain Wiccan beliefs suggest that there is a fifth element which is called spirit. In this particular case, it is represented in the intention with the witches casting spells. This means that it is present.

If you are new to the world of magic and aspire to be a witch, you need to be aware that the use of candles as part of Wicca rituals does not mean that you will receive an instant solution to your problems or that objects such as money will magically appear while you rest. Therefore, you must take your time with your daily life and spirit work along with your efforts to ensure that you have the highest quality of your life. The energy shifts ensure that you will get more, provided you apply some commitment and discipline to your work.

Fire is believed to be a powerful connection to the energy of life, just as in Wicca it is linked to the gods and the voice of God. Since fire is required to be present for offerings to be offered to the gods, the act of burning the offerings is seen as the work of the gods consuming it. Its creative and destructive qualities are significant, and one must try to harness only its positive power. In order to effectively communicate to the flame, you must follow these steps:

1. Launch the Circle

The first thing to do to connect with the fire element is to create a bow. Wiccans use an athame for this work. An athame is an extremely sharp and pointed tool, and usually has a black handle. The athame is usually used for the sole purpose of making circles, and is believed to be the best tool for attracting positive energy and spirits. After you have cast the circle with the sword, it is an affirmation that only energy that is positive is present and that any negative energy will not be able to escape the circle to enter. As you cast the circle make sure there is something in the center that symbolizes the person you are so that you are connected to the energy it contains. Whatever you choose, make sure it aligns with the fire element.

2. Connect with your elemental representation

Once you have finished drawing the circle, you can bring your chosen symbol to rest in the center. When you are finished you can begin to contemplate or make sure you are aware of your surroundings and the things they represent. Breathe deeply and inhale as you visualize your essence. You could also speak words that invite the fire into your life and space. You can also run your fingers over objects or look at them intently. Imagine the item being consumed by the flame, and then how it will prevent you from being consumed in the process. For example, if you have chosen a cloth object, you can imagine that it is magical and that the fire will not harm you as long as you keep it inside you. Also, think about the particular emotion that this item triggers in you to make sure you are able to be more connected to it.

3. The fire element roars

Invoking an element can be the most crucial aspect of connection and that involves talking about it in a way that you can see it, or as if you were face to face. You need to be positive and open, as well as inviting the elements to join the circle. Here is a simple chant that could be used to bring the fire out into the open. Remember that faith is the most important thing, and that you should not doubt that the fire has heard your chant and is in fact present. Recite the spell as you head south, and light a candle when you invite the element into your space. This is best done when you are in a private space, usually at dusk. If you want to be connected to the flame during the day, it is best to go outside and feel the warmth of the sun on your face. Because fire is believed to be directly energized by the sun's energy, absorbing its heat will increase the likelihood of connecting. It is possible to light a campfire or other light source to look at it with a watchful eye. When you look at it, be sure to feel the energy around you and be aware of its transformation in the environment through visualization. Absorb the moment as you watch the flame burn and work to become part of the energies generated.

4. Closing the circle

When you have finished invoking the fire and connecting with it, you can close the circle. Most of the time, closing the circle means acknowledging the fire element for being present and burning, extinguishing any fire that is still burning and then turning the circle in the other direction from the one you started it. Remove any personal possessions you have brought and place certain tools, including the athame in a safe place.

CHAPTER 2 POTIONS AND HERBS

Potions are created using magical or medicinal properties. Most of the time, the key to their proper preparation is to know the benefits and properties of the various plants. By looking at the potions we have, we will be able to create our first lesson solely from herbs.

To make use of a plant in magic, we suggest enchanting it by holding it in your hands, and imagining that your vision of how "goal to achieve" it will be fully realized. Repeat a phrase or rhyme that sums up the idea; continue repeating it slowly initially, and then increasing the pace until you can feel that energy has been generated and you are sweeping it away. Important tip: If it is necessary to heat or cook the plant, you should not use metal, glass or agate containers, as they interfere with its medicinal properties as well as its magical properties. There are five types of potions, depending on the type of preparation. Now we will see how to make each of them:

* TEA: This occurs when the herb is boiled together with water. The typical recipe is two tablespoons (always use tablespoons unless "explicitly stated" otherwise) of herb that has been dried (or 4 fresh tablespoons) per liter of water. Make sure the lid of the pot is completely covered. Do not sweeten the mixture.

* INFUSION: place your plant in a pot and boil the water in a separate container. Then pour the boiling water over the herb and wait ten minutes. The importance of this method is when dealing with fragile plants or flowers.

* TISANE This is the type of preparation that is suggested when using bark and twigs. Place water in a pot and once it is boiling, add the twigs or the peels. Cover and cook for 5 minutes. Turn off the heat but let it rest for five more minutes.

* Dye: Put the herb in a container with a tight-fitting lid. Add alcohol at 60 degrees°F(15°C) and seal. It should sit for 2 weeks, shaking every day. Then strain and store in an opaque glass jar. It is then diluted to drink (usually 5 to 20 drops per glass). The advantage of using the tincture is that other potions can last up to a day if stored in the refrigerator. Tincture that is stored, in a closed dark bottle, can last for a year.

* MACERATION: Pour the cold liquid into a ceramic container and soak the plant in it. Do this for at least 12 hours, if it is an herb, or for 24 hours if it is an acorn or bark. The strain should be consumed as soon as it is noticed. In addition to its use in herbal potions and salves, it is also used in ruxaria to create oils and salves. This is done by heating the lanolin before adding the fresh herbal juices to the centrifuge. The juice should be introduced through the most consumed skin. Another way to apply it on the surface is to massage the fresh herb with the hands and then rub it into the skin. Or crush the plant with a mortar, using a quantity in boiling water. In these cases we speak of poultice. Here we will examine the medicinal properties of plants. When buying it, be sure to look for the scientific name of the plant, as there are usually several species that share the same name. Store it with dark crystals or in colored containers. Keep it indoors and in a cool, dry place away from temperatures.

If you notice any signs of mold, do not use it. If the plant has been attacked by insects, it is a sign that it can be consumed, as long as you remove the part that has been bitten.

* AGRION: Helps digestion and cough remedies. Prepare an infusion using the leaves in the proportion of one tablespoon of dried herb to 1 glass of water. Consume three times a day. You can also eat two stems a day. They can also help with gingivitis and canker sores. It should not be consumed by pregnant women and, when used in excess, can cause stomach and urinary tract irritation. It should not be consumed by people suffering from kidney disease or ulcers.

* ALFAVA: Reduces sore throat. Infuse a handful of the plant in half a liter of boiling water. Drink it several times a day. It also helps fight coughs: soak 15 grams alfphava be dissolved in a 1 liter of boiling water for 20 min. Drink three cups a day. It improves the lungs and reduces inflammation of the throat. But, as with all drugs, should avoid pregnant or nursing mothers.

* BABOUS : to heal wounds. Make a binder with the pulp crushed in a mortar. Then clean the wound with gauze every day for three times. Be sure to protect the wound from the sun. The juice can also strengthen the hair structure if it is carried through the wires, and then left to act for 10 minutes. The skin should not be consumed.

* Calendula: is a remedy for menstrual cramps. Add a teaspoon of flowers in boiling water in a cup. Let simmer for ten minutes before straining. Consume two cups daily for 8 days before the menstrual cycle. Applied on the skin, it can relieve sunburn, treat fungus and acne.

* LEMONGRASS: reduces anxiety. Put a tablespoon of chopped

fresh leaves in a cup of hot water. Helps eliminate gas, aids digestion and can be used as a mild antirheumatic. It should be avoided by women during pregnancy.

* CAPUCHINHA: To expectorate. Mix 2 tablespoons of fresh leaf in a mortar, then add a cup of hot milk, let stand for some time before straining. Drink a cup twice a day. The "way to begin to cure" colds or flu. Do not use in children under five years of age. For patients suffering from kidney ulcers or chronic kidney disease.

* KNIGHT: to treat nosebleeds. Bring water to a boil and add a tablespoon of the hollow stem, cut into slices. Let it simmer for 5 minutes. You can drink half a cup and then do a nose wash with the rest by blowing your nose. To lower the level of uric acids take the same method described above, but boil it for 10 minutes, then let it cool for 15 minutes more. Drink one cup twice a day. Avoid taking it at night because of its diuretic effects. Breastfeeding and pregnant women are advised not to take it.

* CONFREI: for the treatment of bruises. Boil 1 glass of water. Then add a tablespoon of chopped leaves and cover with a lid and let stand for 10 minutes. Remove the gauze while the liquid is still hot. The purple stain will last more than 30 minutes. Take advantage of the new green leaves. Do not use for more than 10 days. You will love it. Do not use by pregnant women or children.

* INDIAN MARIGOLD to help prevent gingivitis. Steep a teaspoon of clove in boiling water. Allow to heat for 10 minutes before straining while hot. Use two to four times a day. It is a good antiseptic. Do not consume the oil. The oil is not recommended for pregnant women.

* EMBAUBA to treat high blood pressure. Take a tablespoon of chopped dried leaves in a cup of boiling water for ten minutes, then drink it. Not recommended for pregnant women or those suffering from hypoglycemia. It is an occasional laxative.

* JOHN'S WORT: helps to relieve those suffering from depression. Infuse a tablespoon of leaves in boiling water in a cup. Leave it for a few minutes and then go. Drink two cups daily. It is possible to take the herb in capsules prescribed by a doctor. It is not recommended to take it along with AIDS medications. If taken in large quantities, it could cause sensitivity to light.

*HERBS: to treat worms. Put a tablespoon of hermit plants in a cup of boiling water. Let it simmer for ten minutes. Not recommended for use in pregnant women of heart.

- DEVIL'S BOTTLE used to combat gout, rheumatism and arthritis. In half a liter of water, place two tablespoons of chopped slices or tubers, and let it heat. Drink two or three cups of water a day, between meals. Its use is not recommended for pregnant women or those suffering from ulcers. If taken in large quantities can cause vomiting and nausea. Do not drink alcohol at night because it may have diuretic effects. Improves indigestion.

* GINSENG: to relieve fatigue. Create an infusion with 1 cup of water, and a teaspoon of root. Take an infusion at dawn, and another at the end of the afternoon. Helps mild depression. Not recommended to be taken for more than 2 consecutive months or by hypertensive people.

*YELLOW ORANGE: to combat insomnia and to relax. Infuse the equivalent of a cup of water with two tablespoons of flower. For ten minutes, let infuse and remove and strain. Grate honey with a tablespoon and drink before bedtime. It can help reduce cholesterol. People with cardiovascular disease should avoid it.

* LOSNA: to combat lack of appetite or indigestion. Infuse a cup of tea with a cup of water, an ounce of chopped leaves and flowers. Let it simmer for about 15 minutes and then strain. Consume before meals. It is not recommended to be taken by lactating or pregnant women with ulcers or who have convulsions. It can be toxic if consumed by those mentioned above.

*RUBY: to combat gas. Infuse 1 cup of water, and a tablespoon of chopped leaves. Let it simmer for 10 minutes and then strain it. Consume it before meals. It is a muscle relaxant and relieves pain.

* MALLOW: to treat trauma in the hollow. Make an infusion with a cup of water and a tablespoon of herb. Inhale the liquid. It can treat intestinal inflammation. Not recommended for pregnant women.

* PASSIFLORA: reduces stress. Create an infusion with 1 cup of water, and a tablespoon of chopped flora. It will be in effect for 10 minutes, then remove and strain. Drink a cup throughout the day and another before bedtime. The herb is not recommended for those who suffer from drowsiness and hypotension. It is not recommended for use in large doses.

* The COW helps to control the day. Take the tablespoon of chopped leaves in boiling water and leave it for 3 minutes. Turn off the stove and consume three times a day before meals. The plant may interact with antiemetic drugs and may cause diarrhea.

* PITANGA is a remedy for stomach problems. Prepare a tea with

water in a cup and a spoon with a leaf. The tea should be ready in five minutes, then filter. Drink at least three times a day.

* STONE AWAKENER: to eliminate kidney stones. Make an infusion with 1 liter of water and 2 tablespoons of dried leaves. Cover the infusion for 5 minutes and strain it, then drink it slowly throughout the day. It helps in urinary tract infections and various types of muscular discomfort. In very high doses, it could cause a purgative effect.

* Rose fly spots and soft marks. Creams or oils containing at least 3% oil should be used. Drop a few drops on the scar or blemish and massage for about three minutes. They can also be useful to treat burns and stop the development of stretch marks. Not recommended for acne-prone areas of the face.

CHAPTER 3 HERBAL REMEDIES VS. PRESCRIPTION DRUGS

We will look at a number of herbal remedies. We will explore how natural remedies are more effective in treating ailments than prescription drugs. In addition, you will gain knowledge about the difference between the two.

Herbal remedies can be used to treat infections, inflammation and the immune system in general, as well as neurological and psychological problems. There are a wide variety of applications for herbs in the healing field. It is vital to keep in mind that it is not advisable to completely replace modern medicine. If you are suffering from a serious illness, it is essential to have the help of a medical professional. Although herbal treatments can help you a lot in treating your health problems, you have to be aware of whether it is essential to consult a physician.

A combination of magical practices and herbs could promote healing on several levels. The healing power of herbs is not a new concept. In fact, it has been used for a long time. There is virtually no moment during all of time that there is not an herbal remedy that is used to heal people. By combining their magical practice, their healing power is greatly increased.

It is not uncommon to find people suffering from various

ailments consulting an herbalist. This is because they are looking for an alternative to conventional treatment. We live in a world that constantly pushes us to take pills to alleviate whatever problem we have. Pills can lead to unintended adverse consequences. The reason many people choose herbal remedies is that there are fewer negative side effects and the benefits are easily visible. It has also been shown that herbal remedies can promote faster healing, which is more efficient.

Many people also seek out herbalists because they have a different attitude than doctors. They see us as people. They treat our problems as a team. Unfortunately, most doctors look at their patients as a source of income. Doctors also treat people as if they are all the same. In fact, we are composed of the same substances, but that does not mean we should always be treated the same way. The body chemistry between individuals is completely different and it is crucial to make sure that when working on healing the body, this is recognized. Herbalists know this and consequently will be attentive to what makes you yourself rather than lumping you in with other people.

Herbal remedies are not only an alternative to healing, but can also be more hygienic. In the world of modern medicine, there are a number of chemicals and artificial substances that are included. These chemicals are capable of harming the body. Sometimes, they will be able to solve the problem, but our body is not able to manage this issue well. The result can make you feel worse than when you started because of the negative side effects that can occur.

Natural healing was very common in the past. Herbal remedies were often used. Many people turned away from this practice when technology and medical procedures assured them that their method of doing things was superior. Over time, many have come to realize that natural healing is actually an effective way to get around. If we are able to avoid introducing chemicals that are harmful to our body, then why should we bother?

There are numerous herbal remedies that are still used even today to treat ailments in the medical sciences. This is because the medicinal properties of herbs are still relevant. An excellent example is the drug aspirin. Its main ingredient is the shrub. It is the Spiraea plant and aspirin is always made from it. This is just one of many examples of herbs that are still used in modern medicine. It should be noted that the vast majority of medicines used today are made from chemicals, rather than herbal substances.

Practitioners of herbal medicine are of many different types. They all accomplish exactly the same thing, but they do it in different ways. Herbal medicine can improve your health and happiness because of the healing power in energy and vitality that herbs offer. The different herbs used are Native American herbalism, folk herbalism and a host of other practices. Spending time researching all of these will give you the most accurate answer as to the best practices that will be compatible with your beliefs, and provide you with finding the relief you are looking for.

We believe you are aware of the great importance of herbs in the field of magic and also in medicine. The energy contained in these plants can be harnessed to aid in healing inside and outside the human body. No matter if you have mental or physical spiritual problems, herbs can help you recover.

Herbal Remedies for Treating Common Ailments

We have seen the main distinctions between herbal remedies and modern medical procedures, now let's take a closer look at some of the actual remedies that could be used in your daily life. Herbal remedies can be found with a myriad of options, so deciding which one is right for your needs is not easy. Visiting an herbalist and spending time discussing the type of treatment you need is beneficial. They are knowledgeable about herbal remedies and their healing qualities.

The most common ailment we will examine is inflammation. When the body is hit with some type or injury, among its initial reactions is inflammation. Consider the inflammation signal as one to the immune system. It alerts the immune system as to how repairs should be made. Inflammation is a common occurrence, and there are a myriad of various remedies that can be used to combat inflammation without taking a medication prescribed by your doctor. Let's take a minute and examine some of the many options available to manage inflammation on your own.

It's vital to keep in mind that these are just a few of the many herbs that help reduce inflammation. You can get natural remedies for a number of inflammation-related problems. A consultation with an herbalist or discussing alternative solutions with your doctor is a great initial step before making any medical decisions.

Now that we've taken an in-depth look at inflammation, we'll move on to another common health problem. Infections can affect each and every one of us at one point in our lives. When we suffer from infections, it is common to be given an antibiotic such as penicillin or amoxicillin. This has helped thousands of people get rid of infections over a long period of time. While these methods are effective, there are also several natural remedies that can help you cure yourself of an illness. The adverse consequences of these natural remedies are less than the negative side consequences of prescribed antibiotics. As we said before take a look at the different natural remedies to help your body cope with an illness.

There are other herbs that help treat illness. But these two are the most commonly used. The information on the other herbs is not as accurate as the data on these two. Infections can be extremely serious, so consulting your doctor or herbalist to make sure you are making use of the correct herb for your condition is crucial.

Keeping your immune system in good shape is always a great thing. A healthy immune system will help ensure that you don't get sick as often. Your body is better equipped to deal with illnesses like colds or the flu. The stronger your immune system functions, the healthier you will be overall. If you want to lead an ideal life, having a strong immune system is essential. You may be surprised to learn that there are a variety of herbs that help strengthen the immune system. Let's examine some of them.

Naturally, keeping your body's immune system in healthy condition is beneficial to maintaining your health. When you have a robust immunity, fighting infections, inflammation and many other problems is much easier. You'll recover faster and be able to get back to your regular life. Keep in mind that we have only offered a glimpse of the many herbal remedies that are available to boost and strengthen the immune system.

The neurological function or capacity of the brain can be improved by using herbal and herbal remedies. In fact, it is shocking to know that the effect herbs can have on ailments such as Alzheimer's disease is quite dramatic. Cognitive function improves when we add various herbs to our diet. Let's look at a list of several herbs that could help improve your neural performance.

Sage: It has a potent aroma. It is a great way to counteract the symptoms associated with Alzheimer's disease. It has a number of compounds that to improve brain function. You do not need to do anything specific to take this herb. It is a great addition to many different foods. This includes foods such as tomato sauce and chicken. You do not need a precise amount of sage to boost mental abilities. A daily intake of it on a daily basis will pay off with increased levels of cognition.

Combating diseases such as Alzheimer's and dementia can be challenging. Both diseases place an enormous burden not only on the person affected, but also on those who care for them. Being able to boost cognitive performance when suffering from one or both of these problems is an incredible feat. There are many other remedies available to help those who do not suffer from these types of ailments but wish to improve their brain functioning. It is also possible to contact your physician or an herbalist to discuss various herbal treatments to boost your neurological functioning.

Doctors are eager to give antidepressants to patients with mental health problems. They can cause a host of negative consequences. They can make you feel like you live your life in a continuous fog or that you don't care about the things that matter to you. This is one of the main reasons why numerous people turn to natural remedies to combat their mental or psychological problems. There are many different herbs that have been studied to show that they can reduce the symptoms of mental illness. They can be used in various methods, including decoction baths, tinctures and salves.

Preparing your spells and rituals

This can be considered the "life agenda" The main goal is to make sure that your life is going in the direction that is comfortable for you. Incorporating these elements into the book you keep of your shadows can help you seek guidance in achieving these goals when you engage with the gods in ritual. It is possible to continue to add to this as you learn things about yourself as you grow.

CHAPTER 4 PHYSICAL SYMBOLS

I believe that the book of shadows would be insufficient if it did not contain certain physical elements within it. Everything in the book does not contain written text. It is possible to include drawings or images of the earth, such as feathers, leaves, stones, plants, etc. I think the use of physical properties is an ideal way to integrate elements into your book. For example, you can create a page with earth or even set fire to the pages to symbolize fire and earth.

You are probably already used to this, but everything you do in your Wiccan experience is completely up to you. That being said, I suggest that your book of shadows remain in the shadows as a secret, and you don't share it with anyone else. I believe that a book of shadows is a very personal device that witches use to protect their innermost and darkest secrets. If you are aware that your shadow book is private and will not be revealed to anyone else, you are free to write in it whatever you want, without filters. For me, this is an incredibly magical experience, as it is possible to make mistakes, as well as change your mind and even change your values and goals, without anyone holding you accountable. Then, you can review your shadow journal over the years and see how far you have come as a person and as a witch.

As a Christian I wasn't a fan of confessing my sins to the priest, because I couldn't imagine why anyone would want to hear these things. If I really asked God for forgiveness, it would surely be an exchange between me and God. That is why I keep my book of shadows in a very private place. It is a space to share all my secrets and desires without anyone else having access to it, other than me and the gods. I would also suggest having a book of shadows in your home, and small, pocket-sized versions, to take with you to rituals, coven meetings and even to carry with you in everyday life.

Rituals are rituals performed to honor and connect with the gods. They can be performed alone or in covens. If you are a Christian, rituals are like going to church, in the sense that you pray, meet with other believers of your faith, and perform specific rituals and actions that help you get closer to God.

Rituals are used for a variety of reasons. They are usually performed to commemorate Sabbats and Esbats. They are performed for important life events, such as the birth of a baby, or the death of a loved one. Rituals can also be used for self-dedication or initiations to welcome new members into the religion.

Although rituals are a great way to create spells and magic, it is not necessary to be a witch to participate in ritual. The reason for this is that the main purpose of a ritual is to connect with God and the Goddess. Even if you are not a Wiccan, you can participate in a ceremony along with other Wiccans, similar to how non-Christians would be welcome in the Christian church.

If you are a novice it is essential that you understand the art of circle casting as you do not want to attract an evil or potentially dangerous spirit by accident and you are not looking to release negative energy if you make a mistake in the ritual or during spell work. Circle casting is the best method to ensure that you keep yourself and others in the vicinity safe.

As with everything else in Wicca, you can select your own method of casting a circle. There are a few key tips to help you cast a correct one in a safe manner. These methods will be explained in the following paragraphs. If you are a beginner, I suggest you follow these guidelines. As you progress and do more research, you can look for more complex circles or design your own.

The circle can be physically marked such as with candles, twigs, stones or crystals, however it is not necessary. If you decide to mark your circle physically, then you should include placing salt, stones or some other material on your altar or workspace while you are "casting". I will show you how to do this along with the other steps necessary to cast the circle.

CHAPTER 5 THE CASTING

To ensure that your circle is efficient, you need more than just making an imaginary circle using objects. Casting the circle spiritually, rather than physically, is a key aspect, and must be done to ensure that all positive and negative energy is where it should be. Creating a circle can be done in four stages:

The space must be prepared: first, make sure that the area in which you intend to work clears the negative energy. To do this, make an upward motion and then use the broom to clean all debris and dirt from the floor. If you are performing an outdoor ritual, you do not have to sweep the ground, however, removing any excess dirt or leaves is helpful.

Circle: The circle creates a circle in physical form this is the perfect time to mark it. You can take your candles, stones or other objects and create the circle on your altar, or in your work area.

Cleanse the circle: Ideally, cleanse the circle with an image that represents the elements. Mix salt and water in a glass chalice and sprinkle the salt water around the perimeter of the circle. To do this, dip your fingers in the salt water and sprinkle it with a shaking motion. When you are done, use a candle and incense to cleanse the circle with the air and light it.

Self-dedication and initiation

Most likely the first ceremony you will participate in will be the initiation ceremony. It is at this time that your Wiccan journey becomes official by being admitted into the religion. The initiation process is unique to you and will not require adherence to any hard and fast set of rules. Like everything else in Wicca, it is your choice to choose how you would like to be initiated. To clarify, an initiation takes place in the event that you would like to become part of an organization or group of witches. Self-initiation takes place when you are on your own, which means you will be a single practitioner. There is nothing superior to the other, but you can practice both.

Coven initiation

If you are initiated as a member of a coven, you must follow the guidelines they set for you. Before you are initiated, make sure you accept the beliefs and goals of the coven members. This is a crucial first step, as initiation into the coven is taken very seriously, just like baptisms or any other significant statement of faith that is common to other religions.

The good thing about this is that, in contrast to Christianity where you are baptized and then initiated into the faith without understanding it, here you can be sure that you agree with all the practices of values, beliefs and gods that are part of your faith as you progress. The process of being initiated is seen as extremely serious and a commitment to be made. It is like getting married, something you plan to remain an element of for as long as it lasts. If you do stumble upon an occult and decide to join it, make sure you are putting yourself on a path that you would like to follow in the long run.

Many beginners are afraid to join or contact covens. I'm sure I was eager to share my practice with others when I started, but don't be. Today there is the internet, which makes it easy to connect with other Pagans and Wiccans who will welcome you into their community. The nice thing about working with other people is that you can learn dances and songs that are a vital element of the culture, although they are not simple to master online, and they are hard to learn from a textbook!

The practice of witchcraft was not traditionally published in literature or books and was an enumeration of practices passed down by word of mouth. It is by far the most authentic and traditional method of learning witchcraft techniques. There is nothing better than studying from people who have already mastered the art. It can be daunting at first, but meeting others who are part of similar beliefs to your own can boost your faith and allow you to feel like you are part of something bigger than yourself and that is exactly what you are.

Self-dedication

Unlike initiation into a coven, where the guidelines and rituals are set by the coven, self-dedication is the sole decision of the individual and you decide which rituals to participate in, and the length of time you participate in these rituals. It is recommended to start on the path to the Wiccan faith only after having a broad understanding of the deities, values and meaning behind the religion. In this regard, it is generally recommended not to commit until you have studied the art for at least a year and a day.

However, I know some Wiccans who self-dedicate before they have studied for a year and a day.

Your path is entirely yours to choose is completely acceptable, but in my experiences, I have found it much more satisfying to commit to your faith after you have completed a year and a day of study. That's what I did. When I took my first step with the full moon in the presence of God, knowing with certainty that I was leaving Christianity for good and that I had made an extremely informed choice, I can only describe the emotion that came over me that night. I was elated, without doubt or guilt. I knew I would live as long as I lasted as a Wiccan.

Since I had spent all my time studying the religion prior to my decision, I was certain that I was dedicated and committed to this choice. My life now had a new mission assigned to it, which was to live a life filled with humility and dedication to helping my fellow man and the world.

CHAPTER 6 THE USE OF CRYSTALS IN MANY ANCIENT CULTURES

There is no single method of using minerals and crystals for maximum impact. It all depends on the severity of the illness and the individual judgment of the person directing and using the stones. Each natural substance has many uses that can impact the emotional, physical mental and spiritual aspects that make up the human being.

Stones can be placed on or near the body through the chakra points, or by simply placing them close to the skin. They can be placed on the body or used as a method of guidance and concentration in meditation. It is the proximity of the mineral or crystal to your skin directly influences the intensity of the energy, therefore, if only minor healing is needed it is possible to obtain from the stones, without being aware of the process.

Before you start using a healing stone, think about all the alternatives and determine for yourself what type of healing is needed and the method by which it is achieved depending on your condition being addressed at the time.

Listed below are some very effective methods, along with complete instructions for all the practices involved in the treatment:

Jewelry

Body contact

Sleep and environment

Crystal bath

Meditation

Chakra healing

Jewelry

Jewelry is a fantastic way to ensure that a stone stays close to the patient in need of treatment. It can be in the form of a necklace, bracelet or earrings, or even rings, the closer the stone is to the skin the more effective it is. This method is ideal for long term continuous treatment, however, it is essential to ensure that your stone is maintained frequently.

To achieve the greatest degree of benefits the jewel is placed near the affected site or in the area chakra that corresponds to the affected region. The energy is directed towards the targeted area in a more powerful way and will result in a more positive outcome. In addition, any areas that are aligned with the stone and are not controlled by the chakra in question will also be healed and stimulated.

If you design the jewelry yourself, let your inner muse choose the stone whenever possible. It is much easier to do this if you have a collection of similar stones. Although all stones will assist in healing, if your subconscious, (spirit), chooses the stone, then its healing benefits will increase.

Contact with the body

Jewelry is not the only way stones can be carried with you. As simple as putting a stone in your jacket pocket will help promote healing energy. You can carry a small bag with stones, put one in your wallet or purse, or inside a pocket, or attach them to your clothing or cell phone. The closer it is to you, the more potent the impact, but as long as it is next to you, it can reap the benefits of its power.

Sleep and the environment

Placing crystals or minerals around your home will give you the feeling of continuous, subtle healing energy. This is not as effective as skin contact or even using a crystal placed in the same room with him will offer the therapeutic benefits.

Consider where you are going to place the stone and the goals you hope to achieve, for example, if you have trouble sleeping at night, you can place stones with sleep inducing and anxiety reducing qualities on your bedside table or under your pillows. If you have problems with concentration or motivation, place the stone on your desk or near your workplace. Symptoms of depression can be alleviated by keeping the right crystals in your home.

Bath

It may be an odd way to use crystal healing, but you can try adding non-porous crystals to your bath water or around your bathroom after showering.

Minerals and crystals can be emotionally and spiritually cleansing. When bathing the body, we are generally in a state of relaxation, so crystal bathing is very effective. When placed in the bath, the healing energy is absorbed by the water, which gives an additional boost to their inherent properties.

Meditation

A variety of minerals and crystals have naturally relaxing and calming properties. This adds to the healing energy they provide, so taking a stone when meditating could aid healing. Since meditation is about opening up and connecting with your spiritual side, it increases the effectiveness of the stones as your body's energy channels flow and open up.

If you focus on the stone or hold it while meditating, you can direct its energy more effectively and, if you want to go a step further, take advantage of the meditation to recharge the crystal yourself, thus strengthening the connection and enhancing the healing intention. If you choose to wear this stone, the effects of your illness will be intensified, which will help you heal more quickly.

CHAPTER 7 CHAKRA HEALING

Once you know how crystals work and the ways you can use them, you can begin to choose the right crystals for the specific requirements of your needs.

Crystals for balancing the Chakras

Seventh chakra (crown chakra).

The colors associated with the chakra are violet and golden white. Therefore, it is natural that the stones that balance the crown chakra are Oregon Opal amethyst and crystals that are clear. Some people also make use of white calcite or white topaz to balance the seventh chakra. Sapphire and diamond are often used to regulate the frequency of the crown chakra.

The sixth chakra is the third eye.

Indigo is the most representative color of the third eye chakra, so the gemstones lapis lazuli sugilite and azurite have positive effects in finding harmony in the third eye chakra. Blue fluorite and sodalite are two other options to regulate this chakra.

The fifth chakra is the throat.

It is a popular choice because of its lighter blue color the throat chakra also has the same crystals, which comprise sapphire, Angelite blue lace agate, as well as aquamarine. Turquoise blue, calcite and kainite are also common crystals that help balance the five chakras.

The heart chakra, also known as the fourth chakra.

The heart chakras are deeply connected to love. The heart chakra has a number of related crystals. Rose quartz is one of the most sought after, and aventurine, moonstone and aventurine are all well-known stones. In addition, many green colored crystals, such as emerald, jade, green calcite and green tourmaline are useful for this chakra.

The third chakra, the solar plexus.

The chakra that relates to shades of yellow also has crystals associated with it including yellow jasper, citrine amber, topaz and yellow sapphire, as well as golden calcite.

The sacral/second chakra

The most commonly used crystals for the red chakra are ruby jasper, carnelian red garnet, as well as brown and red aventurine.

Root chakra or first chakra

It is famous for its intense red tone. This chakra is benefited by Bloodstone, Red Zinc Plated Tiger's Eye and Obsidian, Onyx, as well as Hematite. Smoky Quartz is another crystal suitable for this chakra.

Crystals are used to treat multiple chakras.

Aside from the crystals mentioned above that are associated with a specific chakra, there are other gems that have other functions, which we will cover later.

Harmonizing the chakras

There are some gems that can be used to align or open the chakras. In particular, you should use chrysoprase, pink kunzite and kainite.

Cleansing the chakras

Celestite and moonstone are effective for detoxifying all chakras. Green fluorite also has rejuvenating properties that help each chakra.

Stimulate chakra energy

Use white or clear crystals to increase the energy of your chakras, especially near the crown of your head. Malachite is a fantastic stimulant that can have the greatest effect on the heart and throat chakras.

The addition of turquoise stone can increase the vibration of all the chakras.

Opening the chakras

Quartz crystal is a very popular choice for opening all the chakras, especially for people who are just starting out. In reality, many crystal enthusiasts keep quartz accessible at all times and rely heavily on the wonderful advantages this crystal can provide.

Crystals that target specific ailments and problems.

While using crystals for the regulation of certain chakras can benefit anyone suffering from ailments that affect those areas, you may need to use certain gemstones to heal chronic problems. If you suffer from any of the ailments listed below, you should consider applying the appropriate crystal to alleviate the discomfort. Keep in mind that you should still place the crystal on the chakra where the problem originates and remember that some crystals are not the same way for everyone.

Recurring headaches

The most effective stones for healing migraines and chronic headaches are amethyst, turquoise, lapis lazuli and amber. Headaches can also be the cause of an imbalance in the solar plexus as well as head energy, so if you are experiencing a slight stomach ache that is accompanied by headaches, you should consider using citrine or moonstone to help resolve the problem.

Drowsiness

Sometimes, insomnia is the result of another problem. For example, if you find it difficult to sleep due to constant worry and stress levels, then you may be interested in using citrine, rose quartz or amethyst to help promote drowsiness. If you suffer from nightmares, it is possible to use the protection of stones such as tourmaline and smoky quartz. In addition, if you use them for healing, you can also place them on the floor of your bed when you go to bed. Labrador can also help promote restful sleep, as it helps prevent unwanted thoughts or feelings.

Energy loss

Most crystals with yellow or red hues can increase energy levels. The most potent are deep red garnet, as well as topaz or golden amber. If you are looking for motivation to use in your daily routine, look for crystals with more intense hues such as jasper and tiger's eyes. It is also possible to empower the chakra system in general by holding a clear quartz crystal in both hands and pointing them upward, and placing a citrine crystal on the solar plexus.

Lack of concentration

Quartz crystals are one of the best methods to achieve mental clarity. In addition, you can use citrine and amber to improve your memory, and lapis lazuli is a great way to enhance your thoughts. Amethyst can also help improve clarity and helps you to be aware of your personal goals. If you're studying for an important exam, check out fluorite, which can improve brain function.

Placing corresponding stones over your chakra points will help you channel the stone's energy to the areas of your body that require the most healing. This allows you to channel intense streams of energy directly into the affected area and concentrate the power of your stone on the specific area.

For best results in the chakra healing process, it is essential that you open your chakras, check that they are free of obstructions and then spend at least 10 minutes in a peaceful state while the crystal or crystals are placed on the appropriate chakra or chakras. Depending on the severity of your illness, you may need to do this every day for a short period of time.

CHAPTER 8 WICCAN PRACTICES

There are many types of magic that witches can use. These include tarot cards, dreams, astrology, and many other techniques. Some are more mysterious than others, but all are efficient, and you need to discover the form of Magick that appeals to you. This will allow you to experience various types of Magick to help you make an informed decision about what types of Magick you would like to employ. Be open to all methods, but you need to find one or two that appeal to you. Also, you can mix various types of Magick. For example, you can make use of crystals and herbs in the course of a spell. Technically, you are making use of multiple types of Magic simultaneously, however, most spells are fluid enough that the distinction is not necessary.

Animal Guide

Animal guides are animal spirits or animals themselves, who guide you through your magickal practice. Animal guides are effective and can help strengthen your defense magick. Animals that appear in the flesh can often bond with the person who is practicing. If this occurs, the animal is called a "familiar".

Astral Travel

Astral travel occurs when your spirit is released from your body. When you leave the body you can experience the world as if you were a spirit, or travel to an astral realm. The astral planes are an incredibly chaotic space that is full of stuff. If you are not in your body, you are linked to it through an unlit or golden cord. If the cord is cut you will be unable to return to your body.

Astrology

Astrology is the magic that results from the movement of the planets, the stars and also the time of your birth. Astrology believes that you can draw parts of your personality from where you were born. The zodiac is based on astrology. Horoscopes are also inspired by astrology, as well as the fascinating study of the stars.

Candle magic

Candle magic involves the use of candles in your ceremony, spell or other ritual. Candles can be used in a variety of ways. You can, for example, place a candle on your altar, or use them as points on the pentacle during the form of a magic circle. It is possible to use any candle to perform your rituals. You must prepare them before use. Most spells require specific herbs to be smeared on the candle. In addition, there are some things that you can incorporate inside the candles. The color of the candle you use should be in tune with the spell you are going to cast. The appendix contains a list of associations of the type of candle you should use to obtain various results.

Crystal magic

Crystal magic involves the use of crystals to create your spells. Like candles, however, crystal magick does not require a crystal, but different types of crystals come with different associations that can be used for different purposes. The successful execution of your spell depends on you using the right crystal.

Divination

The practice of divination involves being able to see and interpret the future. There are a variety of divination methods: running on the ground or throwing stones at runes, and relying on the movements of the stars and planets. All of these techniques are called divination and are equally effective. Another effective method for divination can be found in tarot cards, especially when asking questions about the future.

Dream Magic

Dream magic is magic that can be performed while in a dream or similar trance-like state. While you are dreaming you have access to dream worlds. The dream world, which is like the astral realm in that both are made up of mental energy. Using the power of dreams, you are able to influence the thoughts of others. This can be used to direct them towards the outcome you desire. But remember that taking away someone's choices is considered black magic, so it is essential not to force them to do anything that is too intense.

Elemental Magic

Elemental magic is a form of magic that makes use of the five traditional elements: air, water, fire, earth, ether and spirit. Elemental Magic can be a strong form of Magic. If you are going to perform Elemental Magick, make sure you have your magical tools to help you control the energies. Elemental Magick has many associations with Tarot cards, candle crystals and other relationships.

Folklore Magick

Folk Magic is a type of Magick that is passed down from generation to generation. Hereditary Wiccans such as Gardner and Sanders were witches who were born into the family and were initially introduced to the art by their relatives. Folk magic is often performed in the home and is part of common practices such as the use of smudge sticks. But, although it is known as normal magick, it should not be assumed to be any less complicated or effective.

Herbalism

Herbalism is the art of Magick through the use of herbs. Herbalists often make use of a mixture of herbs to make salves, or potions. Herbal magick is extremely effective, however it does require some skill to master. If you are good with plants and herbs, this could be the right option for you. It is possible to have an area to grow all the plants and herbs you require for your magical practice.

High Magick

High Magick is a very ritualized form of Magick. High Magick uses more ceremonies and rituals than other types of Magick. That means that when you cast your spell, you have to adhere to the rules of the ritual exactly. Any deviation could have consequences. This is an excellent choice for those who love to do intricate Magick.

Low Magic

Don't be fooled by the terms low magic and high magic. Both are no more complex or powerful than one of them. However, the difference lies in the amount of ritual involved. High magick involves a lot of specific rituals and ceremonies, while low magick uses fewer rituals and relies on the creation of your own spells and the spontaneity of your imagination, creativity, rather than complicated instructions. Many solo practitioners practice Low Magick.

Petition Magic

Request Magick is the process of receiving Magick as a reward for the services of an entity, divine spirit or other being. Request Magick can be extremely powerful and, in essence, is a way of exchanging services with the entity for a favor from that entity. It can take the form of signing an agreement with the entity, and signing it on their actual behalf. It is essential to know what you expect from petition magic as numerous entities may attempt to manipulate you.

Runic stones

Rune stones can be described as a method that allows you to ask a question and receive an answer. In this scenario you pose your question and then cast the runestones. The meaning of the runes is different for each one and also their location and whether they are up or down. Each of the stones provides a different interpretation to the question.

Sympathetic Magic

Sympathetic magick is magick that creates a connection between the person performing the act and the object. This type of magick is known as transmutation magick since it is possible to take certain characteristics that an object has and use them in different objects. Examples of something that is sympathetic include Tarot cards, crystal ball and any other magical device that has been connected to the user. There is a darker side of sympathetic Magick found in voodoo dolls as well as Black Magick. Charging objects can be charged by either white Magick as well as Black Magick. Beware of using magical tools that are connected to a different practitioner.

Talismanic Magic

Talismanic Magic is when a witch wears a talismanic amulet, or ring, that she wears. Talismanic Magick is like sympathetic Magick but the object is usually something that has continuous Magick that is constantly on. Talismanic Magick is very useful for protection spells, protection spells, and invisibility spells.

Tarot Cards

Tarot cards are made up of 78 cards. They are divided between those of the Major Arcana of independent and significant cards, and those of the Minor Arcana, which are cards with suits. The four suits are Cups, Swords, Clubs and Pentacles. Tarot cards are used to read the future. The person receiving the reading must ask questions. The cards are spread out on the table, in a certain order, which is called a spread. Each card has a meaning based on the card and the place it occupies in the spread, as well as whether the card is reversed or upside down. There are a wide variety of spreads, but the most popular include the three-card spread, as well as Celtic cross spreads. Tarot cards are generally friendly in nature, as the witch is linked with the Tarot deck.

In collaboration with the Moon

The role of fire has played a part in our spirituality since we first discovered fire. There are some myths about the negative effects of candles and candle burning is an integral part of every religion.

Candle magic is often complex, there are certain times that are ideal for specific candles, and there are specific times in the phases of the moon that are ideal for using specific affirmations. Different energies can be repelled or attracted by the color of the candle. These are the most effective times to use candle magick to attract the things you would like to attract.

Mondays and Fridays

Throughout history the heavens have played an integral part of our religion. The planets have been named after Roman gods. They have been based on Greek gods. There is a planet that is linked to each of us. The color symbolizes the characteristics of each planet. To invoke the ancient energy of spirituality people light candles that have the color related to their intentions.

* Sunday

Sunday means that it is the time of the Sun. It is a good day to get rid of negative energy. It is also a good day to attract healing energy. The most beneficial colors to use on Sundays are white or orange and yellow. You can also anoint your candle with lavender or sage oil.

* Monday

Monday is the time that is associated with the Moon. The Moon symbolizes feminine energy This is a perfect day to plan communication. Reconciliation is most effective on Mondays. The colors for Mondays are the colors of the Moon, such as gray and white. Lavender or oils containing ylang-ylang can be used to saturate the candle.

* Tuesday

Tuesday is ruled by Mars, known as one of the Roman gods of conflict. The desire for courage and the wish for your loved ones to return home safe and sound are good intentions to take on Tuesday. It also symbolizes physical challenges and the strength to face challenges. The candle color of choice for Tuesdays is any color of red. Ginger oil and clove are the most effective for anointing your candles.

* Wednesday

This is the day of Mercury, the messenger of the Roman gods. As such, it is an ideal day to make plans related to communication, business transactions and information seeking. Burn yellow, purple or gray candles for Wednesday. Use frankincense or patchouli oil to apply an oil to candles.

* Thursday

This day is controlled by Jupiter. It is a great day to gain fortune and wealth. It is also a good day to perform candle magic in order to attract energy that will heal. Farmers can light candles on Thursdays to increase the likelihood of a healthy and bountiful harvest. Burn blue or brown candles and then anoint them with rosemary or lemongrass oil.

* Friday

This day is under the dominion of Venus, known as the Roman goddess of sexuality and love. This means that Friday is the ideal day to indulge in candle magic with regard to love, partners and relationships. Pink is the most appropriate candle to burn on Friday. Ylang-Ylang oil is the best choice to anoint your candle.

* Saturday

This day is ruled by Saturn. It is the perfect day to set goals that will bring about major transformations in your lifestyle. It is also a great day to seek intuition oriented contact with spirits. For those who want to find lost objects, you should do so on Saturday. You can light a candle in blue, purple or black candles. Be sure to anoint your candle with sandalwood oil or incense.

Phases of the Moon

Most people believe that the Moon has an impact on energy fields that can alter their lives.

The New Moon is also known as the "Dark Moon." This new Moon is the initial phase that is closest to the Sun in the view we have from Earth. It is not common to observe the Moon at this time, unless it is silhouetted during a solar eclipse.

How can this new and full Moon help in candle magic? You should keep in mind what phase the Moon is in when performing candling.

The waxing Moon is the time when the Moon waxes from new to full. This is the ideal time to plan your intentions around attraction. If you are looking to get a job, more money or find a new love it is essential to candle during this time. It is, in essence, the perfect time to do to increase your results.

The slow Moon is the time when the Moon shrinks after a full to new. During this period is the time to make candles to help you plan for the move. If you want to prevent events from happening, you should use candles to prevent things from happening. This is the ideal time for any plan that has to do with protection. It is, in essence, the ideal time to perform candle magic in hopes of diminishing the effect.

The New Moon is the perfect time to set new goals and begin new initiatives. Lighting candles during this time can help you get a fresh start and a new perspective on life.

After the Moon finishes its journey it is full. This is the time when we can celebrate all that we have accomplished. It is important to be grateful for all that we have accomplished. Candle magic takes place at the full moon, with the goal of enhancing communication skills, self-improvement and motivation.

The power of candle magic is beyond most people's comprehension. We have learned that on certain days and in a specific moon phase, are the ideal times to perform candles to attract the things you desire.

Getting the spell set

It is important that you first choose an appropriate color to represent the outcome you desire. You should carve your astrological symbol as well as names on your candle. You can also create runes, seals or sigils. You can also draw an image or write a phrase. You can place an offering at the bottom of the candle, between the candle and the holders. The offering can be honey or herbs. If you want to add some sparkle, decorate the carvings with glitter. Be sure to use the right shade.

You can also decorate the outer supports of the glass if your candle pillar is contained in one. Print images on the internet, use vintage greeting cards or even cut out images from magazines and glue them onto the glass. It is possible to display them as an arrangement on the glass. You can burn or break the edge of the images to make them look natural. You can create the magic spell using parchment and then glue it on the frame. Make sure the images are placed under the top edge and on the side of the glass so that they do not ignite.

Before lighting the candle, be sure to wash yourself with a bath of Epsom salts. Focus your attention on your target. Once you are ready to light the candle, sit down to ground yourself and visualize your intention before lighting the candle. If you need to blow out the candle in the future, that's okay. Relight it when you are ready to do so, but be sure to follow the same steps: cleansing, grounding, etc.

Full Moon Magick

The impact coming from this Full Moon can be felt for three days before and for three days after. Use this time to do magick in the area of the pursuit of success, growth, fulfillment and achievement, as well as blessing and anointing your equipment. If you are looking for more than one oil, herb or color, any or all can be used effectively.

* Strength

Herbs: thistle, St. John's wort, saffron

Oils: Patchouli, Cedarwood Pine

Planets: Mars, Sun

Candle Colors: Gold, red, orange

* Purification

Herbs: lemon verbena, cedarwood, aniseed

Oils: myrrh, olive and incense

Planets: Sun, Saturn

Candle Colors: White, black and rainbow

* Peace

Herbs: myrtle, morning glory, cedarwood, aniseed

Oils: tuberose, magnolia, benzoin

Venus and Jupiter, Jupiter and Saturn

Candle colors: black, pink and white

* Love

Herbs: cardamom, moonwort, basil

Oils: rose, clove, jasmine

Space: Moon, Pluto, Mars, Venus

Candle Colors: red, green, pink

* Health

Herbs: mullein, larkspur, coriander

Oils: myrrh, sandalwood carnation, eucalyptus

Space: Moon, Pluto, Mars, Venus

Candle Colors: green, pink, light blue

* Friendship

Herbs: passionflower, lemon

Oils: Sweet pea

Jupiter, Venus and Moon

Candle Colors: Brown and gold.

* Energy:

Herbs such as pine, rosemary.

Oils such as citrus

Mars, Sun: Mars, Sun

Candle Colors: Gold and red

* Use

Herbs "Devil's Cord".

Oils: Cinnamon

Planets: Mercury, Jupiter, Sun

Candle colors: brown, orange

* Success

Herbs: yarrow, verbena, fennel

Oils Bay

Jupiter, Mercury, Saturn

Candle Colors: Green and orange, gold

* Manifestation

Herbs: Heather or mugwort

Oils: Heliotrope

Planets: Jupiter, Sun, Uranus

Colors of the candles: Orange gold, green, red

"Herbs of happiness: Lavender and rosemary.

Oils: Sweet pea

The planets are: Jupiter, Venus, Sun

Candle colors: yellow, pink and gold

* Abundance

Herbs: allspice, mustard

Oils: Cinnamon

Planets: Jupiter

Candle Colors: green

New Moon Magic

This is the best time for cleansing and elimination. It is also a good time for meditation and divination.

* Protection

Herbs: nettle, mullein, rue

Oils: myrrh, patchouli and myrrh, cypress

Planets Neptune, Pluto, Saturn, Mars

Candle colors: Black gray, indigo

* Negativity in liberation

Herbs: rue, holly, fennel

Oils: Basil

Pluto, Neptune, Moon, Saturn

Candle Colors: Silver purple, white and black

* Divination

Herbs: Five anise leaves, five leaves

Oils: sage, incense

Planets: Mercury, Neptune, Uranus

Candle Colors: lavender, yellow and gold

New Moon Magic

The following list can be used at any time of the full or new moon.

* Contacting the spirits

Herbs: mace, dittany, lily root

Oils: basil, frankincense, bay leaf

planets: Mercury, Saturn, Neptune, Pluto

Candle colors: indigo purple and black

* Psychic power

Herbs: verbena, mugwort, mace

Oils: sandalwood, anise heliotrope

Planets Pluto, Moon, Neptune

Candle colors: White and purple black

* Meditation

Herbs: chamomile, benzoin

Oils: jasmine, nutmeg Hyacinth

Planets: Pluto, Neptune, Moon

Candle Colors: Silver white, silver, indigo

As always, make sure your candles are kept in a safe area and don't let a lit candle go unattended. Be sure to give thanks to the goddess.

Starter Grimoire - Spells for every occasion.

A dream pillow that can be prophetic for dreams.

* Lemon balm

* Cinnamon

* Wormwood

* Angelica

* Cup herb

* Rowan

Make equal portions of each plant and mix them together (at a minimum, 2-3 tablespoons of each). Cupwort is by far the most important ingredient in the mixture, so be sure to include it. If you prefer, you can add other herbs to help you dream prophetically. Mix the ingredients and make an incantation bag with silver, black or purple cloth or stuff a pillow of the same color. Place the pillow of your dreams under the one you are resting on.

Spend a week getting in touch with the dream pillow and the magical process you are working on. In the following time (it may be less, but try to give yourself at least this amount of time) make sure you keep track of your dreams and write them down in a dream journal. You will notice a change between the clarity and intensity of the dreams, as well as how well you remember them. You should keep this for about a month before going to bed with your dream pillow so that you can evaluate any changes in your dreams. You should also be able to identify any elements that are prophetic. If you have slept without your dream pillow for about 1 month, you can create a new pillow and repeat the process as you would like.

Your chalice overflows with riches.

Three green stones (preferably those associated with abundance and prosperity).

Fresh whole milk

* Your chalice

A slice of fresh basil * A slice of fresh basil

Fill your chalice with fresh milk. As you fill it, imagine that your life is filled with abundance and overflowing with wealth. Once you have filled the chalice, add the stones into it one by one. As you place them in the chalice, shout in your mind, "My life is overflowing and I have everything I need. So be it. Stir the milk using the basil spring in an upward clockwise direction for three turns after you have added each stone.

Once you have completed the three additions of stones in the chalice and have stirred the milk using the basil spring once more for 3 more turns in a clockwise direction. The basil should remain in the milk, and repeat the incantation a second time. Place the chalice inside an open window under the illumination of the moon for the night. The next morning, take the chalice outside and pour it on the ground in front of the growing green tree to offer as an offering. Place it in the shape of a triangle over the area where you have poured the milk. Leave the sprig of basil in front of it, on the stones. In a short time your life will be filled with prosperity.

Spells with candles to obtain positive energy

* A cauldron or other fire-proof container

* Pencil

* Paper

* Lavender oil

* Jasmine oil

* Pink candle

* Your favorite fresh flower

Start by anointing the candle with the jasmine and lavender oils. Start with one oil and then anoint the entire candle, follow with something similar with the other. Pause to feel the scent of the oils on your fingertips as you work to make the candle. If you want, you can create symbols like hearts and suns (or anything else that makes you feel happy, as well as look happy and smile) inside the candles. When you have finished smearing the candle and have lit it, light it. As it burns, it's a good time to list three things that cloud your happiness right now. Think about them as you write them down.

Next, use the candle to put the piece of paper in the fire and let it burn in your cauldron or other fireproof container. As it burns, imagine your problems being purified and erased from your life by the power of the fire. Once it has completely turned to ash, put some more of the oils on your fingertips and apply them to the flower. Breathe deeply and inhale the aroma of the flowers and essential oils. As you do this you will feel full of joy, and then you will see how happiness replaces your sadness. Put your flour in a glass placed on your altar. Then, take the ashes from the paper on the side of a plate in your vase. Keep this as a reminder of your magic spell. Breathe in the scent of the flowers whenever you need an extra boost of joy throughout your day.

Love ring

- A glass of wine, or sparkling grape juice.

* A new silver ring, which has been cleaned and has never been worn by you.

* A white square

The spell must be cast during the period when the full moon phase is in full effect, so you must be prepared and wait for the full moon to occur. Moonlight is also essential, so it must be a cloudless night in the sky. Take a walk outdoors with the wine and the ring, as well as the cloth. Cover the ring with the cloth and then watch the moonlight shine through the bundle and infuse it with energy. Dig an insignificant space (or put in a small pot of soil if you don't have room to make an opening) and then place the bundle in the soil before wrapping it.

Spend some time reflecting on the areas of your life in which you are looking for love and the particular characteristics you want to attract for those who may be attracted to that area. Don't limit your charm to romantic love alone, as this could limit its effectiveness. Consider enhancing the love you feel within your life in general and romantic love could be an element of this. Pour the wine or grape juice over the freshly covered lump and say, "Goddess, accept this offering from me. I want my existence to be filled with true love." Wait for a month and then place the ring in the earth during this period. At night, on one of the full moons you may open the ring and remove it from the material in which it was wrapped. When you have done this wear the ring on a regular basis to attract the love you desire into your life.

Amulet of protection

* Black ribbon, string or yarn

* A container to keep the amulet in (something like a necklace or key chain is a great way to do this).

* Powdered rosemary

* Five black colored stones (preferably those associated with protection)

Make sure you have a clear area on your altar and then place the stones on the five points of the pentacle. Once placed on the altar, place your focal point in the center of the circular shape they form. Next, connect the ribbons to the stones to form the shape of a circle, starting at the top. Place the ribbon under each stone to serve as an anchor point. Once you have made the circle, you can begin to create a star inside it, to create the pentacle. When you are finished with the pentacle, say "Imbue the amulet with love and allow whatever it holds to do the rescuing" three times as you trace the outline of the pentacle with your fingers, athame or wand. Imagine a glowing bubble appear around the pentacle, then around the object. Place the pentacle on the table for 24 hours before taking the amulet. Do not unroll the pentacle until you have removed the amulet.

Bath to attract luck

* Pine oil

* Basil oil

* Sea salt

* Cinnamon oil

* A silver coin

* Patchouli oil

Take a bath to warm up. While the water is heating, add equal portions of each oil to the water, about three drops of each. When you have added each of the oils to your bath you can take another drop and apply it to the coins with that oil. When the tub is full, place it in your hands and soak for at least 20 minutes in the tub. As you soak in the tub, imagine that you are enveloped by the golden and green sparkles that emerge from the water. When you have finished bathing, take the coin home in your pocket and do not spend it. After a month, donate the money to a person in need, so that the luck will be passed on and continue to bring luck into your life. This spell is particularly effective when used before an event where you need luck, such as an interview or a difficult meeting.

Health and vitality

- A green candle

* A cinnamon stick

* Your favorite drink

* Apple juice

* Cinnamon oil

You have to sprinkle the candle with cinnamon oil and then light it. Next, you can put the apple juice in the chalice. It is recommended that you choose apple juice made from natural apples and with less sugar and additives, as it can be harmful to your health, and processed foods are not good for your health. Next, take your cinnamon sticks to mix the juice clockwise three times. As you do this, you can say, "May health and wellness come to me through the rules of three times 3." Consume your juice slowly and steadily. Be sure to keep the cinnamon stick and grate it. Sprinkle a little cinnamon over your meals whenever you feel unwell or sick. Please note that this remedy is not intended to be a cure, but is meant to enhance prescription or over-the-counter remedies to improve the effectiveness of these remedies.

Sanctuary Spell Bag.

You will need:

Blue colored bag or a square of cloth.

* Blue thread, ribbon or blue string

* Dried chamomile

* Dried lavender buds

Dried lavender buds * Chamomile oil

* Lavender oil

* Angelica root

This spell bag is designed to bring peace, calm energy into your home to make a place of refuge from stress for you. Stress can take over your life and everyone needs a place to relax and be at peace. This spell will bring positive energy into your home while keeping negative energy away. Start by mixing all the ingredients in your cauldron or other container. Add a few drops of each of the oils to your herbal blend in equal amounts. Next, you can select your angelica root and divide it into three parts and then add them to the mixture of oils and herbs. When everything is well blended, take a moment to breathe in the aroma and then add the bag or square of cloth. Next, say, "By the cloth and the blue string, may peace and joy be with the people around you." Next, hang the bag in the entryway of your home or in the area where you spend the most time, so that the scent spreads throughout your home.

If you want to take your time and slowly create your altar, you can gather your tools and plant an amazing herb garden and wait until the time is right to immerse yourself in the realm that is Wiccan magick, that is also acceptable. There is no wrong way to honor yourself with Wicca. Select the path that is right for you.

Conclusion

I have shown you ways to use herbs in Wicca as well as spells so that you can perform them in your Wiccan practices and I hope you find them helpful and turn your life into a magical Wiccan life.

Printed in Great Britain
by Amazon